Patterns of Agile Practice Adoption
The Technical Cluster

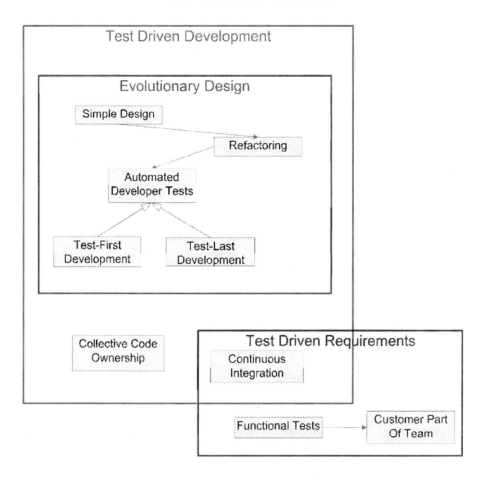

Amr Elssamadisy

C4Media, Publisher of InfoQ.com.

This book is part of the InfoQ Enterprise Software Development series of books.

For information or ordering of this or other InfoQ books, please contact books@c4media.com.

Managing Editor: Floyd Marinescu
Cover art: Nasser Elssamadisy
Composition: Adam Mehling

Library of Congress Cataloguing-in-Publication Data:

ISBN: 978-1-4303-1488-2

Printed in the United States of America

To Samiha and Maha

Thank you.

Acknowledgements

I want to sincerely thank all of the people who have been part of putting together the ideas that went into this book.

First on the list is my wife Maha who has been encouraging me, pushing me, pulling me, and generally getting me to write. She also has spent hours of her time editing this book and many of the papers and articles I've written this year leading up to this book.

Next on my list are Ashley Johnson, Dave West, and Ahmed Elshamy with whom I spent two and a half days in Arizona in the spring of 2006 during the ChiliPLoP conference discussing patterns, Agile practices, and adoption. The four of us shared our experiences over the years and put them in pattern format. After that initial work, Ahmed helped me run a workshop at XP2006 where we presented our ideas and gathered more data for the patterns from over 40 practitioners around the world. Ashley spent countless hours discussing the ideas and refining the ideas in this book.

Dave and I took the ChiliPLoP work and refined it to present at PLoP 2006 where it was reviewed yet again by another group. Special thanks to Ademar Aguiar for taking the time and effort to shepherd our work for PLoP. Linda Rising and Mary Lynn Manns have also read earlier versions of this work. Richard Gabriel led the workshop that reviewed this work, the reviewers were Donald Little, Rebecca Rikner, James F. Kile, Till Schümmer, Lise B. Hvatum, Joseph Bergin, and Guy Steele.

Jean Whitmore co-authored a paper with me earlier this year that was the basis for the *Functional Tests* pattern and *Test-driven Requirements* cluster. Special thanks to Jason Yip for shepherding this pattern and helping us refine the work for presentation at PLoP. The group that reviewed this pattern included Ralph Johnson, Jason Yip, Hesham Saadawi, Dirk Riehle, and Paddy Fagan.

The patterns collected in this book are the result of my own experiences and those of many others. This work would not have been possible without the participation of the people who were willing to spend their time, share their knowledge, and struggle to find the commonalities in the ChiliPLoP workshop, XP2006 workshop, and XPDay Montreal 2006 Open Space session (in alphabetical order):

Soile Aho, Görge Albrecht, Walter Ambu, Giovanni Asproni, Emine G. Aydal, Meir Ben-Ami, Gilad Bornstein, Filippo Borselli, Ole Dalgaard, Ian Davies, Vasco Duarte, Emmanuel Gaillot, Gabor Gunyho, Janne Hietamäki, Mina Hillebrand, Ashley Johnson, Kan Karkkainen, Tuomas Karkkainen, Maaret Koskenkorva, Krisztina Kovacs, Juha Laitinen, Andreas Larsson, Mikko Levonmaa, Youri Metchev, Aivar Naaber, Paul Nagy, Keijo Niinimaa, Loua Nordgvist, Virva Nurmua, Marko Oikarinen, Jukka Ollakka, Paolo Perrotta, Dimitri Petchatnikov, Ron Pijpers, Aussi Piirainen, Ilja Preus, Timo Pulkkinen, Niko Ryytty, Abdel Aziz Saleh, Aki Salmi, Meelis Salvvee, Timo Taskinen, Olavi Tiimus, Ingmar van Dijk, Jussi Vesala, and Daniel Wellner.

Filippo Borselli, John Mufarrige, Ron Jeffries, Floyd Marinescu, Deborah Hartmann, and Kurt Christenson took the time to read drafts of this work and give their feedback to make this a much better work than it was originally.

Finally, thanks to Floyd Marinescu and Deborah Hartmann from InfoQ for giving me the opportunity to write this book and make it available to the public.

Amr Elssamadisy
Amherst, Massachusetts
December 9, 2006

Table of Contents

Foreword by Ron Jeffries

Amr has drawn us a map and shows us how to use it. This book is a travel guide for your software projects.

A few years ago, when my wife, Ricia, and I were traveling in Italy, we spent a few days traveling with Martin Fowler and his wife, Cindy. They didn't know their way around any more than we did, but they are experienced travelers, and Martin is an excellent map reader even in the most hectic Italian traffic. In our few days with them, we saw more interesting sights, had more fun, and got lost much less often than when we were on our own. And after Martin and Cindy left us, we did better because we had learned from what they had showed us.

Whenever we travel in an area we don't know, it's great to have a guide who knows the area. When there's no guide available, it helps to have someone who understands how to read the maps, tracks, signs, and indications. When we're on our own, it helps to learn how to do those things ourselves.

Software projects are always traveling in areas they don't know. Parts of them will be familiar, and we'll do well in those areas. Other parts will be less familiar, and we'll need help. Agile projects, especially when we are just starting out with Agile, offer familiar-seeming situations, but Agile thinking often would have us approach those situations in new ways.

Agile projects center on the delivery of business value, and that's where Amr begins. He describes various kinds of business value, and helps us select our own organization's business values.

Amr then moves on to helping us to identify business and process "smells," indications of things that may be going wrong. This section reads to me like the story of my life in software. I've seen all these things go wrong—and so have you. The good news is that next, Amr is going to help us improve those areas!

Amr helps us improve, first by identifying which Agile practices help us reach the business objectives listed earlier, and by identifying which Agile practices help us resolve the trouble areas. He is telling us how to get where we want to go, and how to deal with trouble along the way. He closes this section by helping us decide which Agile practices we should adopt at the beginning of our project, based on what we most need to accomplish.

Once our project is under way, are we on our own? Not at all. All that I've talked about so far is in the first twenty percent of the book. Now, in Part Two, Amr describes the technical patterns that make up the fundamental activities of developing in the Agile style, including testing, *refactoring*, and more. Each pattern comes with a description of the business value of the pattern, and a story showing how it fits into the process. Then Amr describes the context for the pattern's use, and the forces we'll feel acting on us in the situation. He helps us recognize what we need to do, and how to get started doing it.

Finally, in Part Three, Amr talks about pattern clusters. He gives examples of how the separate patterns work together, providing a stronger and safer approach to delivering value than just using individual patterns separately.

Just as there's nothing like an experienced guide, or an experienced traveler, when you're traveling in a new area, there's nothing quite like having an experienced coach with you when you're traveling for the first few times into Agile software development. If you can get a coach, by all means do so.

With or without a guide, you still need maps and books on how to travel. Amr has written the travel book for Agile, and if you're still finding your way with Agile, I suggest that you bring this book along on your journey.

Agile is a great way to do software, and I hope to see you along the trail somewhere. Enjoy this book!

Ron Jeffries

Foreword by Craig Larman

The adoption of Agile methods and practices, such as Scrum, Agile Modeling, and Test-driven Development (TDD), is rapidly accelerating. Yet 'adopting fast' and 'adopting *well*' are most definitely not the same thing! Many confuse the heart of 'Agile' with *practices* rather than *values*; yet the essence of Agile methods is the four values ("People and interactions over processes and tools," ...) described in the Agile Manifesto. As a result, when they try to adopt a concrete practice (such as TDD or a daily Scrum meeting) various problems arise because they are focused on the surface practice, which is situationally dependent, rather than the underlying principle that guides and informs the adoption of Agile methods. At their heart, adopting an Agile method is about a change of values and principles— a change of mindset—not about a specific practice.

A critical, related point is that Agile methods are meant to be adopted by a self-organizing team where "developer controls the process" (to quote Jim Coplien)—where the team itself decides what to adopt, and how. Yet increasingly, we see "top down" mandated or forced adoption of these methods or practices ("You will adopt Scrum"). These are signs of people not understanding the core values and principles of the Agile Manifesto, and instead, focusing on the myriad surface practices that may support agility. This is a grave mistake.

Amr understands that mistake, and he understands how to help people successfully adopt concrete practices while being informed and guided by the deeper vision of Agile values. You can save time, money, pain, and suffering by following the skillful advice that Amr shares in these patterns, honed through his years of coaching and collaborating with other coaches.

Craig Larman
Chief Scientist, Valtech
Denver, Colorado

Is This Book for You?

Are you adopting one or more Agile practices or seriously thinking about trying out one or more practices on your team? Have you read any of the Agile methodology books on Extreme Programming, Scrum, or Test-driven Development and are theoretically convinced of at least trying the practices?

Or perhaps you're coming off your first project and you've been asked to join another team to help this group succeed as you have done previously. Of course every project is different. So, are the same practices you used last time going to be as effective on the next project? It depends! This book will help you get past "it depends" in order to determine what practices should be adopted as well as give you some hints on how they may need to be adapted.

Maybe you are unlucky enough to have been part of a failing Agile project (or possibly are still on one). Read this book to get an idea why the practices you are using may not be applicable. Be Agile about your Agile practices.

If any of the above scenarios fit, then this book is for you. It will help you look at the individual practices, their relationships, and give you a strategy that has been used several times on multiple projects by multiple companies successfully. It will also give you warnings of how practices have gone wrong before and how you can recognize and respond to the problems that occur. This is not just one person's opinion or an untried method. The patterns you will read here all come from several *real world* project experiences.

Finally, this book isn't for:

- Advanced practitioners who already get Agile practices and are looking for new theories or practices. All of the information here is collected from experience of multiple projects—so chances are you've already heard about everything here.
- Beginners who want to start from zero. This book does not adequately describe the practices from ground zero. It is a good companion to other works that delve more deeply into full Agile practices.
- Those only interested in the non-technical practices of Agile development. These are important practices but they are not covered.

Introduction

In this book you and I will focus on adoption of Agile practices. I will help you answer basic questions that are on your mind:

- Where do I start?
- What practice(s) is best for my particular environment?
- How can I adopt these practices incrementally?
- What pitfalls should I watch out for?

The Plan

In addition to providing the guidance to answer the above questions, I will give you more questions that you should consider and answer on your journey in adopting Agile practices. Does this sound too good to be true? It isn't really. Many of us who have been in the Agile community for several years have figured this out the hard way—by trial and error. This book shares those experiences. Here is an overview of what you will be able to accomplish by reading this book:

1. Focus on business value to the customer. List important areas of value to many customers. An example of a business value would be "reduce cost."
2. Identify symptoms that occur when business value is not being delivered. I'll call these symptoms "smells." An example of a smell related to the 'reduce cost' business value is "customer asks for everything including the kitchen sink." Tie these business values and smells to individual Agile practices.

3. Use the information in 1, 2, and 3 to decide which practices to adopt in order to increase your business value and remove the smells present at your company. At this point you will be able to come up with a coarse-grained adoption strategy for your environment.
4. Provide a detailed description of each practice in pattern format and include adoption information for each practice.
5. Call out practices that work very well together as clusters. Relate these clusters to business values and smells also. Describe the clusters and adoption strategies.

Scope

This book covers an adoption strategy in Part 1 that is applicable for all development practices. Parts 2 and 3 cover technical practices and useful groupings of those practices which I'll call "clusters." To keep the book small and timely, I've restricted coverage of the practices to:

- Automated developer tests
- Test-last development
- Test-first development
- Refactoring
- Continuous integration
- Simple Design
- Functional tests
- Collective code ownership

And the clusters to:

- Evolutionary design
- Test-driven development
- Test-driven requirements

Other practices such as *Iterations*, Stand up meetings, Customer part of team, and others are not covered in this book. Many of them are briefly described in the appendix Patterns of Agile Practices Referenced But Not Defined.

How to Read this Book

So, enough about what you are going to do, how do you do it? The first thing you have to do is come up with a set of Agile development practices for you and your team. You can do that by reading Part 1 (which is less than 20 pages) and taking the time to do the exercises at the end of each chapter. It is very important that you spend the time to solve the exercises. After completing these chapters you will have a list of prioritized practices to consider.

At that point you can start with the second part of the book, which includes the patterns and clusters of Agile practices. You will use the list of practices on your list to "dig deep" by reading each pattern and deciding if it is *really* applicable to your environment. When you find a practice that matches, then you and your team will start adopting it incrementally using the guidance in that pattern. You'll also watch out for symptoms of that practice going bad by using the guidance in the smells documented in each pattern.

Finally, you'll continuously evaluate the effectiveness of the practices you've adopted and adapt them to obtain greater value for your organization. Start right now by turning to the next chapter.

Part 1:

Business Value, Smells,
and an Adoption Strategy

So, you are interested in Agile development. Why? Chances are you want to improve your software development process. Why? Many will answer "to build better software." Again, why is this? Why do you want to build better software? In the Agile community, our focus is on the customer—we want our software to deliver more value to our customers.

In this part I will focus on the idea of delivering more value to customers. Not all customers value the same things. What does your customer value? The chapter on Business Values will introduce several common business values that customer's find important. After reading this chapter and doing its exercises you will have a solid understanding of what your customer values. This knowledge will help you choose the practices to adopt to deliver the most value to your customer.

The focus of this book is on adoption. Not everyone will adopt new development practices to improve the current status. If you are like me and only look for new solutions when there is a problem, then the chapter on Smells is for you. Read this chapter to get an idea of what things smell like when a software development process goes wrong. Do the exercises at the end of this chapter in preparation for creating an adoption strategy that will alleviate your team's pains.

The final chapter in Part 1 is entitled Adopting Agile Practices and shows you how to use business value and smells to successfully adopt a set of Agile practices that will address issues that your customers value. At the end of this chapter the exercises will lead you into creating an initial, prioritized list of practices to adopt tailored for your environment.

1

Business Value

Delivering value to the customer is the main driver for all Agile development practices. How many of us know concretely what specific values are most important to our customer's business? How many of us know what business value is delivered by the software development practice we use? In this and the following chapter I will show you how you can answer these questions and use those answers to decide what practices you should adopt.

In this chapter you and I will examine different areas of business value. The remainder of the chapter is a simple list of seven of the most common business values and their description. Read them to get an overview of what customers find valuable.

The exercises at the end are a necessity—if you really want to adopt the correct Agile practices then do the exercises. The exercises will lead you into discovering what business values your customer finds important.

Reduce time to market

Reducing time to market of developing software brings more value to the customer because they can begin to use the product earlier. A company producing the software can start to earn money earlier if it is a commercial product. This is straight-forward.

Furthermore, consider this: would your customers find any value in partially delivered functionality (e.g. two out of a possible five use cases)? Often your customers will be able to get some early use out of a subset of functionality that you can deliver early rather than rolling everything out in a single release. So not only is the overall reduction in time to market valuable, but frequent, incremental releases can also increase business value and utility.

Practices that help you and your team release early and often provide business value to customers who are concerned with time to market.

Increase value to market

Software development involves taking abstract requirements and building a system to satisfy those requirements. Going from the abstract concepts to running software is a type of invention—the development team comes up with a solution to meet the business need. However, there are multiple possible solutions that can conceivably meet the business needs. Which one is best? Practices that help make this decision correctly create business value.

So how do you determine which is a better solution than the other? Ultimately it is the most useful software to the customer. Does it help them do their job better? Practices that help the customer determine what the better solution is and communicate that to the team correctly will deliver business value as well.

Finally, increasing value to market is related to reducing time to market. Products that get to market faster have the potential of getting market feedback earlier. So there is an opportunity for the team to increase the product's usefulness to the customer by frequently incorporating concrete feedback. Practices that help you and your team take advantage of this information will also increase the value to market.

Increase quality to market

Quality to market has to do with issues such as defects, usability, and scalability. These are probably the most visible issues to your software development team. Practices that help improve these issues increase the business value delivered.

Increase flexibility

How easy is it to respond to changes in business direction? This is the business value behind the buzzword Agile. It is an increasingly important issue in today's market. So, for example, if tax regulations change in one state where your financial software is being used, you need to be able to modify your software to comply.

This value is not always directly visible to the customer. The lack of this factor appears in other business values like slow time to market, or low quality to market. So why do I describe this as a separate value? The notion of flexibility—of being Agile—is one that more and more businesses are aware of directly. Customers want to know your ability to respond to changes they request.

Practices that help your software development effort adapt to business changes will increase the business value that you can deliver.

Increase visibility

This is the customer's ability to see the true state of the project as it progresses. This is important because it allows the customer to steer the software project and also manage risks and expectations.

Lack of visibility results in the customer's surprise and disappointment when a project doesn't meet its deadline. This in turn, engenders lack of trust, blame, and CYA[1] cultures.

On the other hand, software practices that increase visibility will allow customers to get the most benefit throughout the project development cycle and engender trust and cooperation with customers.

---

[1] For readers not familiar with this acronym it stands for 'cover your ass' and is used to indicate a state where someone is focused on avoiding personal blame instead of providing value to their team.

Reduce cost

Faster, better, cheaper. That's what we must all do to survive. We've already covered faster (time to market) and better (quality and value to market). This business value is about building the system for less.

Some of the costs associated with software development include man-hours to build the system, maintenance of the system over time, and hardware as well as software platform costs. Practices that reduce any or all of these costs without equally sacrificing quality will reduce the overall cost of the system.

Another way to reduce cost is to write less code. The 80/20 rule says that roughly 20% of the product is used 80% of the time. Practices that help a team build only what is needed in a prioritized manner will greatly reduce the cost of the product and provide business value to the customer.

Increase product lifetime

Longer product lifetime directly affects the product's Return on Investment (ROI). Unfortunately, software tends to age poorly. Maintenance becomes more difficult and it acquires inertia. Companies that support multiple aging versions of a product spend a large amount of effort keeping those products alive and then finally have to discontinue support because of the cost.

For many product companies this is an important business value to address. Many of the Agile development practices will improve the maintainability and flexibility of the code base that, in turn, increases the ability of the development team to keep the product alive. These practices that directly and indirectly increase product lifetime have business value to the customer.

Theory to Practice: Determining Your Organization's Business Values

Answer the questions below to get a realistic understanding of what business values are important to your customers and organization. Once gathered, share with others—there is a good chance they are not aware of this information.

1. Which business value factors are most important to your clients? Rank them.
2. Invite your business customers to rank the importance of the business value factors. How do their rankings compare to yours? What might you do differently based on the business' rankings?
3. What other business value factors are key in your business? After answering this yourself, ask your business customers. (Some examples are "personal growth" and "supporting open source development.")
4. Given your awareness of business value, are you focused on issues that increase business value? Are members of your team aware of where business value really lies? If not, then by all means, spread the word!
5. Given the information you discovered above about business value factors in your organization, how can you adjust your practices to deliver greater value to your customers?
6. For each business value come up with at least one way that you can take a measurement of progress made. That is, if you are to implement a practice to improve a particular business value you will need to take a periodic reading to verify that the practice is working. This does not have to be quantitative. It may be qualitative in nature. Make it as simple as possible. For example, if you want to take a measurement to reduce cost, a simple (and rough) reading would be the number of hours put in for a major release.

2

Smells

The Agile community has adopted the word "smell" as an indicator of something that has gone wrong. Smells are indicators that business value is not being delivered where it should be. They are a useful concept when deciding what issues need to be addressed and in what order. It is more natural for many to recognize and respond to painful issues (smells) than to put in the effort to improve working processes.

The relationship between smells and business value is not necessarily a one-to-one relationship. Every smell is a symptom of one more business values that can be improved. Conversely, every major business value that can be improved will cause one or more smells to be present.

In this chapter I will introduce two different types of smells. Business smells are smells that can be perceived by the customer. Process smells, on the other hand, are only visible to the development team and not to the customer. Even though they are not visible to the customer, process smells have a direct effect on the business value delivered.

The remainder of this chapter contains a listing and description of several business smells and process smells. These are your indicators that something is not right with the development process. They are good starting points in determining what practices should be adopted—namely those that will be effective in removing the smells. Read through the smells in this chapter and see if you recognize any of them within your organization.

As always, please take the time to do the exercises at the end of the chapter to tie the ideas in this chapter to your organization's environment.

Business Smells

Business smells are the flip-side of the business value coin. They are the pains that a customer experiences when the software does not meet the need. Listed below are five common smells and their descriptions: The descriptions are written from the development organization's perspective.

Quality Delivered to Customer is Unacceptable

Our customers are not happy with the quality of our product. In fact, we have a hard time getting them to upgrade to our latest versions. They have, unfortunately, learned by experience that upgrading to the latest version means having to deal with several bugs that we didn't catch. We are losing customers and getting a bad reputation in the market. We have to be able to deliver better quality code. It is beginning to affect our bottom line.

Delivering New Features to Customer Takes Too Long

We are having trouble adding new features that our customers request. It takes too long to add a new feature, fully test it, and then deploy it to our customers. Competitors have added new features faster than we can keep up—we are losing the race. Our release cycle is long because of many issues that just can't be changed:

- Features rely on expert resources that are bottlenecked.
- The testing cycle takes significant time.
- Features required were unforeseen and are hard to add given the existing architecture.

Features Are Not Used By Customer

Our studies show us that many of the new features we add are not used by our customers and are ignored. This has happened because of several compound reasons:

- Customers didn't know what they really needed at the requirement phase—we therefore built the system upon wrong assumptions.
- Our organization's marketing department sometimes proxies for customers. Requirements from marketing are just a forecast. The forecast isn't always on-track.
- Some features are used much less frequently than we anticipated. We believe this is an indication that our priorities are not in line with the customers' priorities.
- Developers have been known to add features that they were sure would be useful but were not.
- Requirements changed.

Software Is Not Useful To Customer

Our software has not really helped them do their work in a more efficient manner. In fact, we are flooded with usability complaints. There are key functional areas that are incomplete. This is not our fault—we built what were told to build in the requirements. To be fair it is not our client's fault either. She told us what the problem was. We both didn't know how to solve the problem completely when we set the requirements in the beginning. We only learned later but then it was too late—we were already committed to the requirements we had set earlier.

We now have a system that we've spent time and effort building and for which our clients have paid . The end-users are frustrated and see our software as a burden rather than a useful tool.

Software Is Too Expensive To Build

The software process is very expensive. The costs for building a successful project involve a large number of highly-paid professionals over several months (sometimes several years). The value returned on each of these projects does not always validate the amount of investment we put into building them. We are losing much of our business to developers overseas, where the cost is significantly cheaper (but this comes with its own set of serious problems).

Process Smells

Process smells are symptoms of internal software process problems. They are not visible to the customer. They are indirectly related to business value because software process problems negatively affect the business value delivered to the customer.

Process smells are generally easier to diagnose than business smells. But, because they are not directly related to business value, they should not be the main drivers of adoption. If you find one of these smells then relate it back to its business value(s) to ensure that you address the smells with the most important business values for your organization.

Us vs. Them

Those customers don't know what they want! Those developers never give us what we need when we need it. The testers are not team players—they just don't understand how crucial it is to deliver on time. Marketing always promises things that we cannot possibly deliver. Do any of these sentiments sound familiar?

Software development involves an incredibly diverse set of people. If they are blaming each other then problems are exacerbated. Each individual sub team—the developers, the customers, the testers, etc.—will optimize for their team and not the business value(s) which the organization needs. This wreaks havoc with the organizations goals and achievements. Us vs. Them at any level indicates that there are communication barriers and that business value is not on the radar. The most successful teams, Agile or traditional, have a "whole team" mentality.

Customer Asks for Everything Including the Kitchen Sink

The relationship between customers and software development organizations is not always based on trust. In fact, the typical situation today is that the requirements are done upfront and there is an official sign-off as a contract. Any new requirement changes must be put through an extensive change-management process that puts an extremely high barrier on change requirements. The end product may satisfy the requirements 'by the letter of the law' but do not meet the customer's *real* needs.

Customers understand this. Therefore they ask for everything they can possibly think of because they know they have one chance of getting it right. This smell indicates that we are not giving the customers exactly what they need and not giving them the opportunity to learn, refine, and really find out what they need and want. In the end all participants pay dearly. Business smells like *software is too expensive to build*, and *features are not used by customer* result because there is not enough feedback for the proper system to be built.

Customer—What Customer? Direct and Regular Customer Input is Unrealistic.

Scenario 1: We are a product company. We do not have real customers available to us. Our marketing team is our pseudo-customer. They are separate and have their own work to do. They cannot (will not) spare the time to be part of the development team. So they work with managers who in turn work with their underlings who work with us, the development team, to build the correct functionality.

Scenario 2: Our customers are the business members of the company,; we are their support. They do not have time to work with us. Every so often they will spend a little time with us and we take notes. We have their contact information and are free to contact them by email and have regular meetings. This is good enough. They are busy people and it is our job to build the software.

In both of the above scenarios, there is little customer input. This is a process smell that is highly related to leads to the business smells: *features are not used by customer; software is not useful to custome;,* and *software is a burden to use.* That is, to solve the right problem, constant customer input and feedback are required.

Management is Surprised—Lack of Visibility

Management has very little visibility into the *real* progress of a project's development. Development teams are optimistic—despite the fact that several pieces have had problems they are sure they will be able to pull things together at the last minute with heroic efforts. Unfortunately, the details of what might go wrong are not only unknown to management—the development team members themselves aren't quite sure. *Integration* is coming up in a few months time. The development team knows it will be painful but not exactly how painful.

Of course when the actual deadline rolls around, and the team can no longer deny that the deadline will be missed, it is too late for management to respond effectively. This happens all too often and management has learned to buffer any promises made by project teams; a lack of trust evolves.

Bottlenecked Resources (Software Practitioners are Members of Multiple Teams Concurrently)

In order to get the best quality of software, all members of a development team are encouraged to specialize their skill-set. The side effect of this is that these skills are almost always needed in more than one place at a time. A few key practitioners become bottlenecks in the progress of more than one project. It is also difficult to move members of the development teams to other projects. This results in members of the organization assigned to multiple development teams concurrently. That's the nature of the beast when you are in a large organization and there are multiple projects to complete—isn't it?

There is significant research showing that multi-tasking is significantly less efficient than single-tasking. Working on multiple projects concurrently is a much less productive use of time. If time to market and ability to respond quickly to changes are important then these bottlenecks must be removed.

Churning Projects

Projects miss their deadlines multiple times. One deadline is missed, then another, then another. Major design decisions did not foresee issues that later surfaced. The project churns as several different attempts are made to deliver useful, high quality software to the business. Sometimes these projects are discontinued, but only after a significant investment. Other times, the project churns away until finally a working system is built.

Hundreds (Possibly Thousands) of Bugs in Bug-Tracker

When a bug is found it is entered in our bug tracking tool and then prioritized. We resolve all Showstopper bugs before release and most of the high priority ones. Anything of lower priority goes to bug purgatory and stays forever. Sometimes in a new release a portion of the medium level bugs are addressed—but many times they are stale by that point.

A large set of bugs in a bug tracker indicates wasted work. The effort is made to find, locate, and identify these bugs—but no business value is delivered until that bug is solved, integrated, and finally released to the customer. A large number of bugs in the bug tracking system is a direct indicator of a significant investment in work that is never released to the customer and thus has zero value.

"Hardening" Phase Needed At End of Release Cycle

Before releasing code, there needs to be a period where no "new feature" check-ins are made to the code base. The code base must be "frozen," branched, and closely tested. Only high level bugs can be fixed and each one must be approved before doing so. After a sufficient time, typically anywhere between one to three *Iteration*s, the code is released.

This is a good practice right? Why is it under the Smells section? If *Iterations* are done properly—that is at the end of each *Iteration* a working, integrated, tested system is demonstrated—then there should be no need for the hardening phase. The hardening phase indicates that our *Iterations* are not true *Iterations* but are merely time blocks of work. Hardening *Iterations* indicate that the previous *Iterations* let defects go unfound and unaddressed.

Integration is Infrequent
(Usually because it is Painful)

Integration is done a few *Iterations* before releasing because it is a very difficult and time-consuming task. Specialized teams work on the different parts of the application. Documentation and design documents are created upfront to ensure that the parts fit together at release time. Of course they are rarely (if ever) integrated smoothly.

This seems to be the natural way of building applications for most development teams. Although it would be nice to integrate and test the fully working system, it is just not possible. Many of the parts the teams work on will not integrate until the very end. The actual build and link time takes such a large effort that it would be too time consuming to do regularly. What can be gained by integrating more frequently? Why is this a smell?

The lack of *Integration* results in a significant amount of untested code. *Integration* is key to the feedback cycle—without full *Integration* a significant number of errors, miscommunications, and misconceptions remain undiscovered until the end of the release cycle. This inhibits the team's ability to evolve the system as a coherent whole and accurately determine project progress.

Theory to Practice:
What Smells Can You Find?

Answer the following questions to discover, understand, and rank the different smells at your organization:

1. Find as many business smells as you can in your organization. A good place to start would be with your customers, customer-support staff, and marketing staff. They know what is wrong. Rank these smells according to their importance and the amount of pain they cause.
2. Relate those smells to business values. Are they the same business values you identified in the previous chapter as ones that are important to your customer?
3. Find and rank as many process smells as you can. Relate them to business values.
4. Is your smell ranking different than your business value ranking? For example, is the most painful smell related to the most important business value? What does this indicate?
5. Based on your environment, would it be more useful to address value or smells? Why?
6. Re-rank your smells with the information you have just gathered. Is it different than your original rankings? If so, what changed?

3

Adopting Agile Practices

So far you have read about business value and smells. You have also done the exercises at the end of each chapter and come up with a prioritized list of business values and a prioritized list of smells that need fixing. If you have not done so yet then please stop now and go back and do so. Armed with an understanding of your customer's priorities and the main pains your company is experiencing, you are ready to determine what practices you should consider adopting to alleviate those pains and get the most value for your efforts.

In this chapter I will give you direction on how to go about successfully choosing which practices to consider adopting. I'll also ask you to benchmark your work—even if subjectively—so you can be 'Agile' about your adoption. This is, however, only advice on how to come up with your own priorities and your own list of practices to adopt. If you are looking for a prescription—do practice A, then B, but not C—you won't find it here. (And if you do find it elsewhere, my advice to you is not to trust it.)

Pattern to Business Value Mappings

Let's start with the real meat of the chapter. Below are two tables that relate practices and clusters to business value and smells respectively. Use these tables to determine what practices to consider adopting.

Table 1 Practices and Clusters that Improve Business Value

Business Value	Clusters of Agile Practices	Agile Practice Patterns
Reduce time to market	Test-driven Development, Evolutionary Design, Test-driven Requirements	Simple Design, Refactoring, Test-First Development, Test-Last Development, Continuous Integration, Functional Tests
Increase value to market	Test-driven Requirements	Functional Tests
Increase quality to market	Test-driven Development, Test-driven Requirements, Evolutionary Design	Test-First Development, Test-Last Development, Refactoring, Simple Design, Continuous Integration
Increase flexibility	Evolutionary Design, Test-driven Development, Test-driven Requirements	Automated Developer Tests, Refactoring, Collective Code Ownership, Functional Tests
Increase visibility	Test-driven Requirements	Functional Tests, Continuous Integration
Reduce cost	Evolutionary Design, Test-driven Development, Test-driven	Simple Design, Refactoring, Collective Code Ownership, Test-

	Requirements.	First Development, Test Last Development, Functional Tests
Increase product lifetime	Test-driven Development, Evolutionary Design, Test-driven Requirements	Refactoring, Automated Developer Tests, Functional Tests, Simple Design

The table above is to be read by row. Each row represents a business value. The 'Clusters of Agile Practices' column contains an ordered list of the clusters that improve that business value. Therefore to increase quality to market you should consider the *Test-driven Development* cluster first. If the entire cluster is not applicable in your environment or too large a step then consider individual practices.

The 'Agile Practice Patterns' column contains an ordered list of practices that improve that value. For example, if you want to reduce time to market then the first practice you should consider is *Simple Design*.

Pattern to Smell Mappings

Table 2 Practices and Clusters that Alleviate Smells

Smell	Clusters of Agile Practices	Agile Practice Patterns
Quality delivered to customer is unacceptable	Test-driven Development, Test-driven Requirements, Evolutionary Design	Test-First Development, Test-Last Development, Refactoring, Simple Design, Continuous Integration
Delivering new functions to customer takes too long	Test-driven Development, Evolutionary Design, Test-driven Development	Simple Design, Refactoring, Test-First Development, Test-Last Development, Continuous Integration, Functional Tests
Features are not used by customer	Test-driven Requirements	Functional Tests
Software is not useful to customer	Test-driven Requirements	Functional Tests
Software is too expensive to build	Evolutionary Design, Test-driven Development, Test-driven Requirements.	Simple Design, Refactoring, Collective Code Ownership, Test-First Development, Test-Last Development, Functional Tests
Us vs. Them	Test-driven Requirements	Functional Tests
Customer asks for everything including the kitchen sink	Test-driven Requirements	Functional Tests

Customer? What customer?!	Test-driven Requirements	none
Management is surprised	Test-driven Requirements	Functional Tests
Bottlenecked resources		Collective Code Ownership
Churning projects	Test-driven Development, Test-driven Requirements	Automated Developer Tests, Functional Tests, Continuous Integration
Hundreds of bugs in bug-tracker	Test-driven Development, Test-driven Requirements	Automated Developer Tests, Functional Tests, Continuous Integration
Hardening phase needed		Continuous Integration
Integration is infrequent		Continuous Integration

The smells table is to be read and used exactly like the business value table. Empty clusters indicate the clusters do not give an improvement over the single practices in alleviating this smell. Please keep in mind there are many more Agile practices than those covered in this book. These tables only reflect the patterns described in this book.

I have now given you all the pieces of the puzzle to devise an adoption strategy tailored directly to your environment. For the remainder of the chapter I'll discuss how to use these pieces together effectively.

Be Business-Value Focused

Remember that the goal of software development is to provide value to the customer. Respect that. If you do not have access to the customer then you should do your best to get that access. Work with your customer to really understand his or her needs. Use the exercises in the previous chapters to have conversations with your customer. Once you have a prioritized list of business values that are important to your customer, spread the knowledge. Make sure your team is aware of that information. Put it up in an *Information Radiator* for the entire development team to see and remember.

Be Goal-Oriented

I did not have you work hard to determine and prioritize your organization's business values and smells arbitrarily. You will now use those lists to determine the goals for your adoption of Agile practices.

When adopting a practice do so knowing why you are adopting that practice. Are you doing so to reduce time to market? Or is it to increase the quality of the product? Or is it to alleviate the pain of hardening *Iterations*?

Do not make these decisions alone. Involve your customer so that he understand why you are making these changes. Make these decisions with business value in mind. Marketing doesn't care if you are adopting *Test First Development* or not. They care that the product has fewer defects. Let them know that you are adopting *Test First Development* to reduce defects and that you expect them to see results in the next release.

If your adoption is driven by customer needs, and you track your progress in that area (even if subjectively), you may get their support. If you include them in your reviews instead of hiding your faults they may start to trust you and work with you. If you deliver improved results then you'll have raging fans.

Adopt Iteratively

Adopt in small steps. Start with a small team and get experience in adoption. Most small teams that get appropriate coaching make the transition to Agile practices well. Learn as you go. What you have in this book will help, but it is only a start. You need to experience the practices for yourself and build up your own body of experience.

After your first successful adoption project, ramp up to more people and more projects. Share your experiences. Share this book. Take periodic readings of your business values and smells—they will change with successful adoption. Use the information here to help you watch out for pitfalls by recognizing and responding to smells as they appear.

Be Agile About Your Adoption

As you adopt iteratively have periodic retrospectives about your adoption. Use the feedback from those retrospectives to modify your development process. Tweak the practices. Drop the ones that don't work. Adopt new ones to complete a cluster of practices.

Test-Driven Adoption Strategies

You can use the information you have gathered so far about business value and smells to determine which practices you should consider adopting:

1. **Choose practices solely based on business value delivered**. In this scenario there are no severe pains from which you are suffering and you just want to improve your software development process by increasing the business value your team delivers. Use the Business Value and Clusters of Agile Practices in Table 1 to decide which practices to adopt.

2. **Choose practices to alleviate smells that have been prioritized by business value.** This technique focuses on alleviating pains that you have while keeping business value in mind. Smells are prioritized according to the business values that are valued by your customers. Then, from the prioritized smell list, you choose the appropriate practices to adopt with the help of Table 2.

3. **Choose practices to address the most visible smells.** This is common although I wouldn't recommend it. This is plain and simple "firefighting"—trying to get rid of the biggest pain regardless of the business value it delivers. This is all too common when the technical team determines the priority

without the customer's input. (I've often been guilty of this.)

The information found in the tables in the beginning of this section is prioritized by effectiveness. Therefore the first practice in the list is the most effective practice for increasing the business value or alleviating the smell. Get your feet wet with the first practice and after that is successfully adopted come back and take another look at the remaining practices and clusters related to your business value or smell.

No matter how you prioritize your list of practices to adopt you should adopt those practices as iteratively as possible. Armed with the list of practices here is how you can successfully adopt the Agile practices on your list:

1. Start with an evaluation of the status quo. Take readings (even if subjective) of the current business value(s) you want to improve and the smell(s) you want to alleviate.
2. Set goals that you want to reach. How much do you want to increase the business value? How much do you want to reduce the smell? What is the time frame? Take a guess initially and modify it as you know more through experience.
3. Pull the first practice or cluster off the list you created.
4. Read the pattern that is related to that cluster or practice. Decide if it is applicable or not by matching the context and forces to your working environment. (more details on what patterns are and their different sections in Part 2: The Patterns on p. 47) If the practice is not applicable in your environment go back and pick the next one off the business value/smells table.
5. Once you have determined that the pattern is applicable in your environment then read the pattern thoroughly. Follow the advice in the adoption section in the pattern in order to get started.
6. Periodically evaluate whether the business value you are addressing is improving or that the smell you are addressing is

being resolved. If it is not, adapt your practice for your environment using hints from the *Variations* section and the 'but' section in the pattern.

7. Go back to step (1) and re-evaluate your business value or smell. If it needs more improvement (i.e. you still have not met your goal set in (2)), consider adding another practice or an entire cluster to resolve the issue. If it has met your goals then move on to the next one.

So where is the "test-driven" part of this approach? Your tests are your goal values that you set in step (2). In step (6) you check your readings after adopting a practice. This is a test of how effectively the practice(s) you adopted has already met the goal set earlier. This loop—set a goal, adopt a practice, then validate the practice against the expected goal—*is a 'test-driven* adoption strategy.[2]

Theory to Practice: Building Your Own Agile Practice Adoption Strategy

Answer the following questions to build an adoption strategy. (Use the answers from the business values and smells chapter exercises here.) Also, see the appendix entitled Adoption Strategy Case Study for a real world example of how this might be done.)

1. What are your goals for adopting Agile practices? Do you want to alleviate smells or add business value? Be specific. If there is more than one then prioritize them.
2. Take readings of the current business value(s) and smell(s) you want to address. Don't worry if they are subjective or fuzzy. Know, to the best of your ability, where your organization is today with respect to business values and smells.
3. Choose an adoption strategy. Choose practices using that strategy to adopt.

---

[2] In management practices this is commonly referred to as the PDCA cycle (Plan, Do, Check, Act), originally developed by Walter Shewhart at Bell Laboratories in the 1930s and promoted effectively in 1950s by the quality management guru W. Edward Deming.

4. Read the next chapter that introduces the patterns. Then start following the steps outlined in this chapter to adopt your first practice. Don't forget to periodically take readings of your business value/smell to make sure that the practice is effective.
5. Congratulations and good luck! You've started on your path to Agile practice adoption!

Part 2:

The Patterns

4

Introduction

What is a Pattern?

In general, a pattern describes a particular problem and its solution context. Specifically in this book, a pattern describes a (set of) problematic situation(s) on a development team that can be fixed by applying an Agile practice. Patterns are to be trusted because each one has been used several times on real development teams and projects— they are not one-off solutions or 'good ideas' that might or might not work. Patterns are "discovered" and not "created."

The pattern format used in this book is as follows:

Name
Description: a brief overview of the practice or cluster.
{Dependency Diagram:} A diagram showing inter-practice dependencies (for practices) and grouping (for clusters).
Business value: A sorted description of the business values this practice or cluster improves.
Sketch: A fictional story that describes this pattern being used on a software development project in context.
Context: The preconditions and environment where this pattern is useful. The context is a collection of invariants: issues that do not change by applying the pattern.
Forces: Used to elaborate context and give specific issues that are problems (partially) resolved by this pattern. In

49

fact, correct application of the pattern should remove many of the forces.

Therefore: The pattern description.

Adoption: Steps, ordering, guides to adopting this pattern.

But: Negative consequences that can occur from applying this pattern.

{**Variations:**} Different ways this pattern has been implemented successfully other than that described in the *Therefore* section.

{**References:**} Where to read more.

Use the name, description, and dependency diagram to get a quick overview of the pattern. You may find yourself browsing the pattern descriptions and dependency diagrams to get a feel for what the different practices are and how they are related to each other. Read the Sketch to get a big picture example of how this pattern may be used in practice.

If you find yourself considering the applicability of a pattern to your environment then the *Context* is the section for you. This section contains any preconditions that must be met and environments where this pattern is useful. If your environment does not match the context then the pattern may not be effective.

The *Forces* section documents the issues and problems that drive the type of solution that this pattern represents. Similar to the *context* section, use the *Forces* to help you make a decision about whether or not to adopt this pattern. If you find some of the forces present in your project then that is a good indication that this pattern will have a positive affect and will help you resolve these problems.

The next section, the *Therefore* section, is the solution—it is a description of the practice itself. Use this information to understand the practice and its details. But also remember that this book is not meant as a tutorial. If you have no idea what the practice is, you may need to go to other sources to get a more in-depth discussion of the practice.

The next three sections are going to be very helpful in your actual adoption of the practice. The *Adoption* section will give you an incremental strategy to successfully start using this pattern. The *But* section will let you know what may go wrong as you go about adopting a pattern. And the *Variations* section will give you non-standard ways in which others have successfully used this pattern. Use these three sections as step-by-step instructions to help you get to the point where you are practicing the pattern as described in the *Therefore* section.

Where applicable, the *references* section gives you pointers to material where others have documented this practice. Instead of having these references in the bibliography in a jumble for the entire book, each pattern has its own pointers on where to go to read more.

Using Patterns Effectively

There are several ways to read a pattern. Here are some ways that the patterns can be used depending on the situation:

- I am already practicing the pattern. There are no problems. I just want to see how others have used the same pattern.
  - Look up the pattern by name.
  - Read the *Context* to see if you are using the pattern in the same environment as others have done.
  - Read the *Therefore* and *Variations* sections and match them to the way you are using the practice.
- I am practicing a pattern but it doesn't seem to be very useful. Am I incorrectly using the pattern? Or is the pattern just not useful in my environment?
  - Look up the pattern by name.
  - Read the *Context*. If your environment doesn't match the context then maybe you should consider modifying the practice or dropping it all together.
  - Read the *Forces*. Are you trying to solve the same type of problems? If not then consider that the practice might be working but that you need another practice to solve the problems you have in mind.

- o Check out the *But* section. You will find how others have gone wrong and some advice on correcting the problems to get the full benefits from the practice.
- I have problems on my team that I want to solve by adopting Agile practices.
  - o Go back to the chapter on smells and try to match your problems to smells.
  - o Read the practice(s) that addresses that smell.
  - o For each practice:
    - Read the context to make sure it applies to your environment.
    - Read the rest of the pattern.
    - If you decide to adopt the practice then follow the advice in the *Adoption* section.
    - Periodically check for any of the smells documented in the *But* section.
- I couldn't find the problems I want to solve in the *Smells* chapter. Does that mean that none of the practices can help?
  - o No. Read the *Forces* of the individual patterns and see if you can find similar problems to the ones you want to address. You will probably find a match.
- We are adopting a particular practice. Are we there yet? Have we successfully used the pattern to its fullest?
  - o Find the practice pattern by name.
  - o Check the *Forces*. Are any of the problems in the *Forces* still problems on your team?
  - o Check the *But* section. Are any of the smells in that section present? If so, address them.
  - o If none of the problems occur then you have gone beyond what is documented in this book. You probably have enough experience and intuition to tailor the patterns on your own. Congratulations!

Finally, please treat these patterns with a modicum of disrespect. The pattern format is an excellent format to help you tailor your own solution. Every one of these patterns is based on multiple projects using the practices. They are proven in the field several times over. Nevertheless, there is no silver bullet. These patterns will be wrong in some instances. Use these patterns as guidance, but when reality contradicts theory—choose reality.

5

Automated Developer Tests
(Abstract Pattern)

A set of tests that are written and maintained by developers to reduce the cost of finding and fixing bugs—thereby improving code quality—and to enable the change of the design as requirements are addressed incrementally. Disciplined writing of tests encourages loosely coupled designs.

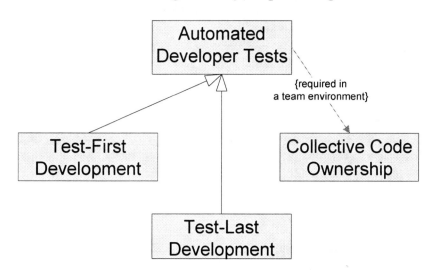

Business value:

Automated Developer Tests help increase quality to market by catching errors early in development cycle. Flexibility and product lifetime are improved by creating a 'safety net' of tests and enabling *Refactoring*. The previous values are obvious, what is not as obvious is that *Automated Developer Tests* also reduce the time to market and cost of development by actually reducing the development time.

Sketch:

Waterfall Will and Uthman UpfrontDesign joined Scott ScrumMaster's Agile development team at the beginning of their third release cycle. Scott's team had two spectacular successes under their belts and some of the developers went to other teams to "spread the Agile disease." Will and Uthman came from traditional development backgrounds where testing was done by the QA department and the only times that developer tests that were written were adhoc tests on an as-needed basis.

As Waterfall and Uthman joined Scott's team they practiced Pair Programming with others on the team who had a disciplined testing regimen. Some of them, like Cindy Coder, would write their tests first and practiced Test-First Development while others, like Dave Developer usually wrote unit tests after doing some coding, but always would have them done before checking into the code repository.

Because Scott's team was a self-organizing team they chose not to enforce writing tests but very highly recommended that developers write tests for all of the code base to support the fact that there were no sub-teams; every developer had access to change any part of the code base.

Uthman and Will ran head-first into this problem as they took on the invoicing subsystem of their application. They paired to incrementally build upon the invoicing system (which unfortunately had no tests) and were very happy with the design and flexibility of the functionality. Aparna Analyst was also very pleased with the work they added and signed off on the work being done and since it passed all her (manual) acceptance tests. Dave and Cindy were pairing to modify how the "charge" object worked (which was heavily used by the invoicing subsystem). They also added their work to the system successfully. As Aparna was preparing her work for the next Iteration she noticed that the invoices produced by the system were no longer working. When Will and Uthman discovered this issue they went to Cindy and Dave and asked, "Why didn't you tell us you were making such significant changes?!" Dave and Cindy replied, "Where were the tests? We rely on tests to tell us if we've broken anyone's functionality."

That was an annoying lesson in one of many aspects of Automated Developer Tests. Will and Uthman played a significant role in the next Iteration, rewriting the invoice work to make it work with the new charge code and adding developer tests.

Context:

There are many contexts in which this particular pattern is effective. Any or all of the following are environments that will benefit from this practice:

- You are on a development project that needs to significantly improve its quality—i.e. reduce its bug count.

- You are on a development team that has decided to adopt *Iterations* and *Simple Design* and will need to evolve your design as new requirements are taken into consideration.

- You are on a development team that wants to build code using a distributed team. The lack of face to face communication and the constant feedback is causing an increase in bugs.

- You are on a development team that is practicing *Collective Code Ownership* and need to compensate for the fact that not everyone knows the entire code base but may touch any part of the system at any given point in time.

Forces:

- Checking in code to the source tree to be tested by QA significantly increases the cost to find and fix a bug.
  - There is the simple fact that now both a QA person and a developer must both find the bug and communicate via a tool to document the work being done.
  - There are also the many times that bugs go back and forth between QA and development until the problem is clear enough to be reproducible.
  - The time for a bug to be found, discovered, and fixed is usually at least one order of magnitude greater than if the developer had discovered and fixed it before checking in the code. By then, other developers have had time to check out that faulty code base and built upon it.
- Fixing one bug frequently causes another bug. Cycles and chains sometimes occur where one bug causes another that in turn causes another, ad infinitum.
- Complex parts of the system tend to have more bugs than others. Their bugs also tend to be recurring because not everyone understands the code base.
- Systems are designed to be general so that when requirements change the system can accommodate the changes. Unfortunately this extra flexibility doesn't come for free—there is a cost to the extra complexity. Every time a developer works with a complex piece of code it takes time to understand it and time to properly use it. This is known as "cost of design carry."
- "Band-Aid" fixes are made because changing the design of the system is prohibitively expensive—if you change something you probably will break something that is dependent on that. This eventually leads to code duplication, poor and brittle design, and less maintainable code. It takes a long time to get it through QA before release, and even then problems get through. Hence we minimize the amount of things our fixes affect out of fear.

Therefore:

Reduce the overall effort for finding and fixing bugs by finding them earlier: have developers test their code more rigorously. Have that testing automated and available for all other developers so they can test for bugs that may have been introduced by their changes but outside of the tests they just wrote. Introduce a practice that has all developer tests running before checking in any code into the source repository. Help make complex systems more understandable by documenting them. Make sure that the documentation changes with the system; the best way to do that is to make documentation executable (i.e. well-written tests). Finally, whenever a bug is discovered, write a test first to reproduce that bug., Add it to the test suite, then fix that bug and check in both the fix and the tests to the code repository. You have now ensured that that particular bug will not come back because any developer who reintroduces it will fail your test and not check in the code until it is fixed.

If you are working in a team environment then eventually some of the code you write may break existing tests. After all, one of the main benefits of a test is to act as a safety net and warn you when you break assumptions made by other parts of the system. Remember that you have to get all tests passing before you check in your code change—therefore you will have to change the affected parts of the system to pass the tests. Both *Collective Code Ownership* and *Pair Programming* are helpful in solving this problem.

By introducing *Automated Developer Tests* and making them easy to run by grouping them in test suites you can address all of the problems introduced in the *Forces* section. Be aware that once you have started writing tests regularly you will see a change in the way that developers attack problems on their team. They will be much more confident and courageous and will make design changes when needed relying on the tests that have been written to catch their mistakes. Therefore you must be diligent in writing *good* tests for all of your code or you might find yourself in the position of Will and Uthman in the sketch at the beginning of this pattern.

What are good tests? That is a nebulous question and almost as difficult as answering "what is good code?" Tests are best treated as any other code—not as a second class citizen—so everything you know about good design should be adhered to. The best way to learn is to start writing tests. Learn by doing. Read what others are writing. Pay very close attention to all the problems that occur and modify your test writing technique to avoid those problems.

Adoption:

We will not cover exactly how to write a developer test—there are many books that do so in great detail. Instead we will cover the steps that you need to perform so that you and your team have the maximum likelihood of successful adoption with this practice:

1. Commit as a team to the discipline of writing tests.
   a. Realize that this is first and foremost a human issue and not a tool issue.
   b. Agree that tests are just as important as production code.
   c. Agree that it is better to miss a feature completion than to have a feature complete without tests.
   d. Agree to be patient. Depending on your current project it may take anywhere from two to six months for this practice to become a habit and for the *real* benefits of *Automated Developer Tests* to become obvious.
2. Find a tool that is easy to use. The ease should be with respect to the amount of effort it takes to write a test and not whether or not you have to write that test.
   a. JUnit and TestNG are available for java. NUnit and Visual Studio's built in testing tool are available for .NET. CXXTest and CPPUnit are available for C/C++.
   b. Use automatic testing tools as auxiliary testing and not the primary form of testing. If you rely only on test-generation, you will lose the thought process that goes along with making code more "testable" and the gain of more loosely coupled, better designed code.

3. Treat your test code as you would your production code. Tests should be well designed also.
4. Get as much help as you can on this.
   a. Bring in an experienced consultant or two if you can.
   b. Try to enlist the help of others at your company who have successfully participated on projects in which they have been disciplined about either *Test-First Development* or *Test-Last Development.*
   c. Buy several copies of books specifically on TDD and xUnit testing. (recommendations provided at the end of this chapter) Encourage your development team to take time to read these books.
   d. Get involved with online communities and local user groups focused on TDD, Agile Development, etc.
   e. Don't worry about Mock Objects and pure Unit Testing initially. (If you don't know what these are then don't worry about it as they are not important at this point.) As a starting point, write tests for each non-trivial method in each class. There is no need to write a test for simple getters and setters.
5. Adopt *Collective Code Ownership* to support team development. This will enable you to always fix tests when they are broken.
6. Consider adopting *Pair Programming* as a support practice to ease the learning curve for the team. It is easier to be disciplined about tests when you are working with someone else.
7. Start writing tests with the current *Iteration.* Expect a slowdown of up to 50% if you are working on a new project. If you are on a project that already has a large amount of untested code your slowdown will be more pronounced. Your testing time will go down over time to about 20%–30% of the total development effort. You will eventually hit a "critical mass" point where existing tests help you write new code. This will speed up your overall development time. Believe it or not you will develop *faster* even with the testing overhead!
8. Within a few *Iterations* your team will come up against the problem of setup data. As you write objects that rely on other objects, that in turn rely on even more objects, the amount of code

written to "setup" for a test increases. There are two approaches to this problem:

a. Pull out the common setup code into common classes. These classes have the responsibility of creating classes and test data—they are a special type of factory. They create business objects in a given state. Martin Fowler gives a brief overview and links to the original ObjectMother paper presented at XPUniverse 2001 here
http://www.martinfowler.com/bliki/ObjectMother.html.
ObjectMother is a common evolution of complex setup code. Your tests are always exercising real business objects (a good thing). On the other hand the ObjectMother creates a maintenance burden and can easily become unwieldy from supporting too many special cases. Tests based on this solution may become brittle because one test relies on many business objects.

b. Use Mocks and Stubs to keep away from the complexity of ObjectMother. Mock objects and stubs are place holders for the business objects under test. They can be used to cut off the thread of one object pulling another several objects for testing purposes. A very good paper describing the correct use for Mocks and Stubs is _Mock Roles, Not Objects_ which was written by the group who created the jMock framework. Mocks can be used to make your tests much more readable and less frAgile. On the down side, mocks are a form of duplication—a proper mock object mirrors the business object it mocks. That comes along with all of the dangers of duplication. If the business object changes then a mock must change also; if it does not then a test will continue to pass even though it should really fail.

9. Both approaches—mocks and ObjectMother—work well. The important part is consistency: agree as a team on an approach and follow it. This will make it easier for team members to work with each other's code.

10. Use Mock objects and Stubs to test classes that communicate with external systems.

11. If you are brand new to this type of development start with ObjectMother to keep from adding too many new tools at once.

After the team is comfortable with *Automated Developer Tests* then the team can shift towards mock objects.

But:

There are several ways that new adopters of this practice go wrong:

- This practice is fragile: it needs everyone on the team to be onboard.
  - If one person breaks a test and does not fix it then it is much easier for others to do so. That one break—usually with a "it's not in my part of the code" or "I'll get to it later"— is the beginning of the end for *Automated Developer Tests.*
  - Developers must get used to fixing tests that they break even if they did not write them. This will mean that they will need to touch parts of the system they are not used to working with instead of creating a bug in the bug tracker and moving on.
- The fact that tests are written says absolutely nothing about the quality of the production code. Badly designed code can be written in any language and in any technique. Tests encourage loosely coupled code and a good developer writes better code using this technique. But bad code can still be written; consider adopting *Pair Programming* or performing regular code reviews of the tests if you have this problem.
- Tests sometimes end up as second class citizens: we break all the rules of good design. What this inevitably ends up causing is brittle and hard-to-write tests. Treat your test code as you would your production code. Refactor it when the design is no longer adequate. Be mindful of coupling and cohesion and all of the other principles you already know and practice.
- Writing tests—especially for existing systems that have been written without testing in mind—is very hard. Don't give up. Figure out how to put in tests incrementally. Be prepared to slow down significantly before you start speeding up again in your

development. Pick up a copy of *Working Effectively with Legacy Code* by Michael Feathers for some suggestions on how to proceed.

- All tests should be running and passing all the time—no excuses. Sometimes teams will check in something that breaks a test. It will not be fixed (we'll get to it later). That one broken test becomes 10 and then 100 and then 400 broken tests within a few *Iterations*. This should be unacceptable. You've just lost one of the major advantages of this type of testing: catching bugs early and keeping other bugs from being introduced based on faulty code. You are also desensitizing your team to broken tests. Fix this immediately: pull out all the broken tests into their own suite. Impose/convince/beg your team not to break any more tests. Any broken tests should force an immediate rollback. Incrementally start to migrate the broken tests over to the functioning test suite by fixing them and then moving them to the live test suite.
- Code coverage becomes an overly important metric. Managers drive from code coverage. Although using code coverage to indicate areas of code that need more attention is valid, using code coverage to drive development is not. It can (and often is) easily "gamed."
  - The fact that a test calls a method says nothing about the quality of that test. Code coverage statistics are often mistakenly used as "test quality" statistics—they are not.
  - The relationship between tests and methods on a class should not be one-to-one but many-to-many if indeed we are writing tests to verify the code's conformance to requirements. Coverage encourages a one-to-one form of testing. Write a method—and then make sure you have a test that exercises that method.

Variations:

There are two types of *Automated Developer Tests* that are patterns in their own right, but they both address the forces described here adequately. This abstract pattern gives a context and a set of forces that can be addressed by both *Test-First Development* and *Test-Last Development*. There is therefore quite a bit of overlap.

Instead of using *Collective Code Ownership* to share code, some teams will adopt *Pair Programming* instead. They have very specialized team members and it is unrealistic for them to have everyone learn enough to modify all parts of the code. Their solution is to rely more heavily on *Pair Programming* and have a culture that encourages this. The problem here is obvious; you've just put more tasks in the lap of some of your bottlenecks. This type of pain needs to be resolved, either by augmenting the staff or by giving in and moving towards *Collective Code Ownership*.

This practice is also known as *Automated Unit Tests* in the community. The reason I've chosen the word "developer" instead of "unit" is that there is a debate whether they should be true unit tests—tests that exercise only one class at a time—or not. It is not important for adoption. In fact, it is easier not to write true unit tests until you get your feet wet. At that point you will have enough information to make your own decision about unit testing.

References:

Automated Developer Tests are discussed in books on Test-driven Development and ones written specifically for JUnit (the leading testing tool in Java). Michael Feather's book listed below is about testing and test-driven development with existing systems:

Astels, David. 2003. *Test-Driven Development: A Practical Guide.* Upper Saddle River, NJ: Prentice Hall.
Beck, Kent. 2003. *Test-Driven Development By Example.* Boston, MA: Pearson Education.
Feathers, Michael. 2005. *Working Effectively with Legacy Code.* Upper Saddle River, NJ: Prentice Hall.
Jeffries, Ron. 2004. *Extreme Programming Adventures in C#.* Redmond, WA: Microsoft Press.

Massol, Vincent. 2004. *JUnit in Action.* Greenwich, CT: Manning Publications.

Rainsberger, J.B. 2004. *JUnit Recipes: Practical Methods for Programmer Testing.* Greenwich, CT: Manning Publications.

6

Test-Last Development (Implements Automatic Developer Tests)

Test-Last Development involves writing tests *after* writing the code to support the requirements for a particular task. They exercise the system as it has already been built.

Business value:

Test-Last Development addresses the same business values as indicated in *Automated Developer Tests*. These values are quality to market, flexibility, product lifetime, time to market, and cost.

Sketch:

When Uthman UpfrontDesign joined Scott ScrumMaster's team along with Waterfall Will they both had agreed to Pair Program with other developers on Scott's team and to do their best to pick up the development practices that the team had adopted. One of those practices was to always create Automated Developer Tests for each and every piece of code written.

After a few Iterations of pairing with others on the team, Uthman and Will paired up on the invoicing subsystem. Since they were new to the Automated Developer Testing practice they planned to write tests after writing some code (i.e. Test-Last Development). So they designed and coded and added to the already existing invoicing subsystem incrementally. It turned out that this was a piece of the code that had absolutely no tests, and since they had already completed the code (close to the end of the Iteration), they called the task done and skipped the tests instead of having the task be marked as incomplete. The next Iteration they signed up for more work on the invoicing system. And unfortunately it came down to the wire and tests were dropped. (This was an independent system anyway, so they weren't hurting anything by not adding tests and as long as they were working on the subsystem it would be alright.)

Therefore, when Dave Developer and Cindy Coder modified a piece of the system that the invoicing subsystem depended on, they ran and passed all of the tests and checked their code. The invoicing system stopped working (silently). Aparna Analyst noticed this as she was running the system to prepare for the next Iteration's invoicing requirements and told Will and Uthman. Needless to say they were upset and when they confronted Dave and Cindy to ask them why they weren't more careful they got a "well our code ran all of the tests. How were we supposed to know your invoicing work would fail?!"

This particular incident cost Will and Uthman a large portion of the next Iteration to correct and back-add the developer tests that they should have written earlier. On the bright side they picked up the habit/discipline of always writing their developer tests. To keep from making the same mistake again they wrote their tests more incrementally—that is after every development step they would write the tests for the code just written.

Context:

You are on a development team that has decided to implement *Automated Developer Tests* and therefore the context from that pattern applies. Furthermore:

Most (all) of the members of your team have no experience with *Test-First Development* and you want to adopt a practice that is not completely different from what they were used to previously.

Or maybe your company has purchased a tool that helps with creating developer tests. The generation of tools for developer testing can only generate tests for code that has already been written.

Forces:

All of the forces in *Automated Developer Tests* apply plus:

• Writing tests for existing code takes a smaller learning curve than learning to write tests *before* writing the production code.

Therefore:

Develop your production code in small steps. After every small step write a developer test using your tool of choice to exercise the code that you have written. Collect the tests that you and others write in Test Suites so that they can be run in groups easily. Do not check any code into the source repository that has not been fully tested. Run all developer tests before checking in your code base to make sure that you have not broken anyone else's tests by your change.

This type of development is not only about tests; it is about the production code that results from this practice. Production code will be, by design, more testable. The "testability" will drive a design that has far less coupling than code written without this in mind. The code produced, including the tests, reduce the cost of change. The design will be modifiable instead of something static that we will only "band-aid" for fear of introducing more bugs than we fix.

Adoption:

The adoption strategy in the parent practice pattern, *Automated Developer Tests* is sufficient to cover the adoption of *Test-Last Development*. Be aware that this is practice is less effective than *Test-First Development* but easier to adopt. Many have used this practice as a stepping stone towards *Test-First Development* to get their feet wet with disciplined testing.

But:

This type of testing is not new. In fact, developer tests written in this manner have been around long before their emerging popularity with eXtreme Programming. In addition to all of the problems in the *But* section in *Automated Developer Tests,* these problems are unique to *Test-Last Development:*

- Testing is dropped during crunch time. Although this is a problem in both *Test-Last Development* and *Test-First Development,* it is much more common here because the code is seen as "done" before the tests are written. *Will* and *Uthman* in the sketch above are not uncommon.
- Testing is seen as an overhead and the practice is sometimes dropped as a whole.
- Tests are biased towards the solution. A developer writes the code which is a solution to the problem defined by the requirements. The tests should logically make sure that the code conforms to the requirements but often makes sure that the code conforms to the code.

References:

Test-driven Development by Dave Astels is a proponent of *Test-Last* development:

Astels, David. 2003. *Test-Driven Development: A Practical Guide.* Upper Saddle River, NJ: Prentice Hall.

Feathers, Michael. 2005. *Working Effectively with Legacy Code.* Upper Saddle River, NJ: Prentice Hall.

Massol, Vincent. 2004. *JUnit in Action.* Greenwich, CT: Manning Publications.

Rainsberger, J.B. 2004. *JUnit Recipes: Practical Methods for Programmer Testing.* Greenwich, CT: Manning Publications.

7

Test-First Development (Implements Automatic Developer Tests)

Test-First Development involves writing tests *before* writing the production code that will support and eventually pass that test. Tests resulting from this practice tend to be a developer's understanding of requirements because there is no "design" at its inception.

Business value:

Test-First Development addresses the same business values as indicated in *Automated Developer Tests*. These values are quality to market, flexibility, product lifetime, time to market, and cost. In general, although *Test-First* and *Test-Last* development address the same business, *Test-First* development is more effective and harder to adopt.

Sketch:

Uthman UpfrontDesign and Waterfall Will joined Scott ScrumMaster's development team earlier this year. As they Pair Programmed with others on their team Uthman and Will got a taste for Automated Developer Tests and had their own run-in with what happens when someone does not write tests for his code on an Agile team. (See the sketches for Automated Developer Tests and Test-Last Development.)

After fixing the invoicing system code that they had coded without tests and back-filling the tests for that part of the system, Will and Uthman decided to do one more Iteration together on some invoicing tasks. They decided to try to write their tests first. While they had done this previously with others on the team on other tasks, they had never led an effort themselves, and so they struggled. It was very difficult and awkward to come up with tests to code that hadn't been written yet. They ended up talking through a design on paper and/or white board, discussing both the static and dynamic structures, and then writing a test for the "virtual solution" they came up with in their heads. At the end of the Iteration they had a very small piece of production code working that was tested. But they were far from happy with their experience.

On the subsequent Iterations Will went back to Test-Last Development and was very disciplined in writing tests incrementally with the production code. Uthman, on the other hand, decided that there was something to this Test-First Development and tried to pair with as many people who were already doing Test-First Development as he could. He picked up a Kent Beck's TDD book and went through the exercises. He "suspended his disbelief" because he saw that there were many people who he highly respected who were using this practice exclusively. He also learned about mock objects via the Mock Roles, not Objects paper and learned to use JMock effectively. After several slow Iterations the light bulb finally went on for Uthman and he was hooked!

The next time Uthman and Will teamed up on a set of tasks, Uthman drove in a Test-First manner and explained to Will what he was doing. When Will drove he developed in a Test-Last manner. Uthman felt that the quality of tests were much better with Test-First Development when comparing Test-First and Test-Last but he kept it to himself...

Context:

You are on a development team in an environment that matches the context of the *Automated Developer Tests* pattern. Furthermore:

- You want to get the most benefit out of the developer tests.
  - o You want to increase your development speed.
  - o You want to increase the benefit of tests in creating and promoting loosely coupled designs.
  - o You want to have full test coverage of your requirements instead of test coverage of the design.
- You may have already adopted *Test-Last Development* and have noticed that tests are not always written—especially during crunch time. Unfortunately this is when you need tests the most.
- Your team is willing and able to struggle through an awkward stage while this practice becomes natural. (Usually one to three months.)

Forces:

Test-First Development resolves all of the forces documented by *Automated Developer Tests*. The following forces are also resolved by *Test-First Development:*

- Tests that are written *after* the code are more likely not to be written. In crunch time it is very easy (and common) for developers to move on to the next development task before writing the tests for the current task.
- Tests written after code drive code indirectly. A developer writing production code keeps the fact that he must be able to test this code in the back of his head while developing. So, in that way, the design is affected by the tests to be written.
- Tests written *after* the production code is written are (usually) biased towards the solution when they should be validating the problem. That is, a developer test should verify that the production code written satisfies the requirements. But when the production code is written first, the developer has already solved the problem and tests written reflect that fact as they exercise the production code. All this really verifies is that the code written works as the developer thinks it should. The requirements have gone by the wayside untested.

- Tests written after code may or may not test all of the requirements that drove that code to be written.

Therefore:

Write your developer tests *before* writing the production code to support the requirements. At this point, since you have not yet solved the problem by writing the production code, the only information available to you will be the requirements. By forcing yourself to write this test you will need to make decisions about classes that will support the required functionality—you will make design decisions to support the requirements at hand. Your test therefore will mirror these requirements and will be a form of "executable requirements." This test should be failing—probably failing to compile too. That is as expected.

You will then write the production code to satisfy the one test you have written. You have already made decisions regarding responsibility assignment to classes and now you only write the code needed to make that test pass. The test you wrote earlier will drive the creation of classes, methods on those classes, and their relationships to other classes in your system (i.e. object oriented design).

Once you have made the test pass you now have a passing test and production code that satisfies the requirements. You have not written one line of code that has not been driven by requirements. If you are strict about never writing code without a failing test to drive that code then you have "requirements coverage"—meaning that you have a test that exercises each and every requirement supported by your code.

The last step is to *Refactor*—that is to modify the structure of your code without changing its behavior. You have the passing test that verifies the behavior; therefore any change that you make that does not break the test you have written means that the behavior is still the same. Do not add new functionality but feel free to clean up any sloppy work and use the existing tests to ensure that the behavior is the same after you've done your cleanup work.

What we have just described is the Red-Green-Refactor loop in the *Test-driven Development* pattern.[3] It is a mandatory part of *Test-First Development*.

Adoption:

There are people who have successfully adopted *Test-First Development* completely by themselves. Many have written about their experiences in online articles, conference papers, and blogs. They are the minority. By far, most of us who have successfully adopted this practice have done so with outside help. Here is how to go about doing this:

1. {Required} Commit to learning this practice as a team and being patient while individuals on your team internalize this practice. Agree to suspend your disbelief for at least two months and plan for a significant slow-down in development speeds of up to 50% (75% if you are on a project with legacy code that was written without tests in mind).
2. {Recommended} Send your developers to a TDD Immersion class.[4] These types of classes are typically 80% to 90% hands on work using the *Test-First Development* approach and other practices under experienced practitioners'/instructors' tutelage. They will give the attendees a good head-start in a controlled environment.
3. {Highly Recommended} Bring in help until this practice catches on (an outside consultant is best, but if you have internal resources who have successfully practiced *Test-First Development* they can carry out this task). You will need someone who has "been there,

---

[3] *Automated Developer Tests* and especially *Test-First Development* are big parts of *Test-driven Development* although they are only part of TDD in a team environment.

[4] Many are offered by consulting companies in open enrollment or onsite format. Check www.valtech.com, www.objectmentor.com , and others. Get recommendations from people you know in the community who have attended any of these classes. Do your best to get into a class where the instructors have real-world development experience.

done that" with respect to these practices. They need to be able to pair with the developers to help them learn this technique hands-on. Typically you will need at least one person per four to five developers for at least one week out of every month for several months. They will be there to keep morale up, show ways that tests *can* be written, and help the team adapt and adopt this practice to your particular environment.

4. {Highly Recommended} The parent pattern, *Automated Development Tests*, encourages that you adopt *Pair Programming*. This practice is very important in easing the learning curve.

But:

This is one of the most difficult practices to adopt of all of the commonly know Agile practices.   All of the problems listed in *Automated Developer Tests* apply here also. In addition this way of development is "backwards" to many developers and very non-intuitive. It takes a significant amount of practice for the light bulb to go on as to why this is a superior method of development. Developers must suspend their belief long enough to figure out how to perform *Test-First Development* efficiently. This practice has a high drop-out rate.

Variations:

Distributed teams use *Test-First Development* as a form of requirements documentation. The tests are written by someone who has face-to-face contact with the customer and then those tests are given to the developers who are to build the production code.

References:

Test-First Development is almost synonymous with *Test-driven Development* in published works:

Beck, Kent. 2003. *Test-Driven Development By Example.* Boston, MA: Pearson Education.

Feathers, Michael. 2005. *Working Effectively with Legacy Code.* Upper Saddle River, NJ: Prentice Hall.

Jeffries, Ron. 2004. *Extreme Programming Adventures in C#.* Redmond, WA: Microsoft Press.

Massol, Vincent. 2004. *JUnit in Action.* Greenwich, CT: Manning Publications.

Rainsberger, J.B. 2004. *JUnit Recipes: Practical Methods for Programmer Testing.* Greenwich, CT: Manning Publications.

8

Refactoring

To *Refactor* code is to change the structure (i.e. the design) of that code while maintaining its behavior.

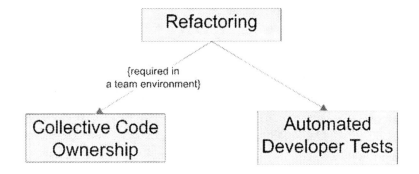

Business value:

Refactoring increases flexibility and the product lifetime by allowing and encouraging developers to change the design of the system as needed. Quality to market and costs are reduced because continuous *Refactoring* keeps the design from degrading over time and thus making it harder to modify the product correctly.

Sketch:

Uthman UpfrontDesign jokingly told people that he was considering changing his name to Rashid Refactoring after a few months on Scott ScrumMaster's team. As he learned about other Agile practices such as Pair Programming and Automated Developer Tests he became aware of an option that has never been open to him before. He could re-design his code when requirements were changed or added. After reading Refactoring: Improving the Design of Existing Code by Martin Fowler and with the Automated Developer Tests present, he learned how to incrementally change the design of his code to accommodate new information.

He no longer put together elaborate designs at the start of a new piece of functionality. This wasn't really as bad as he had thought because he found himself doing a little design each and every day. The practice of Refactoring had quickly replaced Upfront Design as his favorite practice.

Context:

You are on a development team that is practicing *Automated Developer Tests*. You are currently working on a requirement that is not well-supported by the current design. Or you may have just completed a task (with its tests of course) and want to change the design for a cleaner solution before checking in your code to the source repository.

Forces:

These are problems that are a natural result of software development:

- Traditionally, software gains entropy over time. Requirements change, the software is band-aided with less than perfect solutions because of the increasing cost of making a change to the old, frAgile code base.
- Quick fixes quickly build up a design debt that charges interest daily in the form of code that is more difficult to understand and modify.
- Code duplication is almost inevitable in order to avoid changing working code and possibly introducing a bug.

- Requirements are added and/or modified and the current design is no longer a good solution to the problem.
- Software development is a learning process and the design decisions that make sense today are incorrect when seen with tomorrow's information.

Therefore:

Incrementally change the design of the code instead of proffereing a quick and dirty fix. Do not add new functionality *and* change the design at the same time—this complicates the issue. Change the design of the code while maintaining the behavior. Ensure that you are maintaining the behavior by relying on *Automated Developer Tests* and *Functional Tests*. Start with a passing set of tests, change your design, and fix any broken tests by changing production code (not the tests). At this point—from passing tests to passing tests—you have changed the design and maintained the behavior. This process is called *Refactoring*.

Refactoring is a very simple and elegant activity. It is best when practiced regularly—before and after every task. That is, before you start a new task read the existing code and determine if it will support the requirements of the task you are working on. If it does not, then make the necessary change(s) to the design before starting on your task. At this point go ahead and code the task and its tests. After you are done re-examine the resulting design. If the design can be improved then go ahead and improve it by *Refactoring* the design again so that you do not leave any design debt for the next person down the line.

Adoption:

This is one of those "just do it!" patterns (well almost…). One of the things to keep in mind is that *Refactoring* is a practice and not a tool— although tool support helps. With that in mind, here is how you should go about adopting this practice:

1. Start *Automated Developer Tests* until you are comfortable with the discipline of writing tests for all of your tasks. Do not attempt *Refactoring* any piece of code until there are adequate tests covering the particular segment to be modified.
2. In a team environment, adopt *Collective Code Ownership* on your team—agree on how to handle broken tests from *Refactorings* in a timely manner.
3. Pick up a copy of <u>*Refactoring: Improving the Design of Existing Code*</u> by Martin Fowler and a book about Test-driven Development that is exercise-driven.
4. Start. Perform the steps as described above. For every task inspect the design to see if it needs changing to accommodate the new work. After completing the work inspect your own solution and clean it up if needed. Be disciplined in *Refactoring* mercilessly— that is before and after every task if applicable.
5. Run a bi-weekly study-group to share different *refactorings* that have been performed.
6. As you become comfortable with the canonical *refactorings* as defined in Martin Fowler's book, be courageous and make significant changes. Work towards large design changes that you and your team have known were needed when appropriate. Get a copy of <u>*Refactoring To Patterns*</u> by Joshua Kerievsky and run a study group around that book to expose yourself to larger *refactorings*.

But:

Refactoring is one of the most powerful practices in a developer's toolbox. Nevertheless, here are some things to watch out for:

- *Refactoring* delivers no *direct* business value. By definition *Refactoring* maintains behavior, making it completely transparent to users. Therefore *Refactoring* without a requirement that causes the code being refactored to change is wasteful from the Customer's perspective.
- Many missed small *Refactorings* build up over time causing the need for *large Refactorings*. Large *Refactorings* are much more

difficult to perform. Therefore be diligent in constantly *Refactoring* your code and cultivate your sense of code and design *smells*.

*   In a team environment you will eventually *Refactor* code that causes tests that you have not written to break. Some new to Agile practices may check in this code and rely on the developers who have written the tests to fix the broken test. In this path lies the danger of breaking down the *Automated Developer Tests* practice. It is unacceptable to check in code that breaks existing tests. Make sure to practice *Collective Code Ownership* in a team environment so that you are able to make all of the tests pass after performing a *Refactoring*.

Variations:

We know that the majority of the cost of software development goes into maintenance and not the initial creation of a software system. It then makes sense that we focus on making our systems maintainable.

Traditionally we design for tomorrow in mind—that is we build a flexible system so that when new requirements come the design does not have to change to incorporate the new requirements. But there is a hidden cost in this solution: a general design is more complex. We pay for that complexity every time a developer has to understand and use that code. One of the most common techniques for sharing these flexible designs is via Design Patterns. Erich Gamma in his 1995 edition of *Design Patterns : Elements of Reusable Object-Oriented Software* promotes this type of solution.

In an interview in the summer of 2005 Gamma stated that his thinking had evolved and he now starts with a *Simple Design* to meet the requirements at hand. When new requirements emerge he is able to *Refactor* the solution towards a Design Pattern. Therefore he does not have to carry the complexity of the design until it is absolutely needed.

This, of course, brings us to the variation of *Refactoring* towards patterns instead of using design patterns upfront. In this way we merge the benefits of both techniques. *Refactoring To Patterns* by Joshua Kerievsky is full of examples of how to do this effectively for common problems in today's development environment.

References:

Fowler's book is a reference that should be on every developer's bookshelf. Kerievsky's book is useful when you have gained experience in *Refactoring* and want to learn to focus your *Refactoring* toward well known design patterns:

Fowler, Martin. 1999. *Refactoring: Improving the Design of Existing Code*. Addison-Wesley Professional.
Kerievsky, Joshua. 2004. *Refactoring to Patterns*. Addison-Wesley Professional.

9

Continuous Integration

Continuous Integration is a practice of performing a clean build, full integration, and running all tests every time a change is committed to the code repository. This is accompanied by frequent integration of each developer's work into the code repository.

Business value:

Continuous Integration reduces time to market and increasing quality to market by finding *Integration* bugs often and early, thus eliminating "hardening *Iterations*" and the rework that goes along with it. *Continuous Integration* also increases visibility of the progress of the project by making it explicit to the development team and stakeholders.

Sketch:

Bob BuildMaster had been reading about <u>Continuous Integration</u> *and noticed that many of the problems this practice was purported to solve were present in his project. So Bob spent some time over the next several weeks fully automating the build. At that point he ran a nightly build and made the results available on a web page where the entire team could see the results.*

Bob then sat down with Scott ScrumMaster, Cindy Coder, and Dave Developer to show them what he had done and to get their buy-in. They came to an agreement that build problems were to be solved as soon as they were found. Cindy and Dave also agreed to work with Bob to get all of the Automated Developer Tests they had written to be part of the nightly build also.

After a few Iterations the development team started relying on the nightly builds that ran all of the developer tests. The key, they found, was to remove all errors as soon as they were discovered. By doing this the entire team became more aware of integration problems and their causes. Bob also made the build script available to all developers to perform a local integration before checking into the code base.

With that success the team decided to do full Continuous Integration and Bob dedicated a large portion of the next three weeks to installing and configuring a CI tool, reducing the build time to just under ten minutes.

Context:

You are a member of a development team that has decided to reduce the risk associated with "hardening *Iterations*." Or you are on a development team that is adopting *Automated Developer Tests* as a practice and want to keep the build passing all tests. Or you are on a development team that is introducing *Functional Tests* and want to make sure that the team is incrementally adding new functionality without breaking the old.

Forces:

There are many problems in today's typical software development lifecycle that are directly addressed by *Continuous Integration.*

- *Integration* has been traditionally seen as very difficult and risky. This typically drives several practices to buffer against this risk of uncertainty: (These practices are suboptimal.)
    a. Sub-teams work independently and "stub out" work to be done by other sub-teams to avoid the need for *Integration*.

b. Sub-teams start out with a detailed design of their subsystem boundaries to make sure that their subsystems will come together smoothly. (which is almost never the case)

c. Have "hardening *Iterations*" at the end of a development cycle to figure out what mistakes in assumptions your teams have made.

- *Integration* becomes exponentially more risky with time.
- Lack of *Integration* typically masks a large set of bugs. Many of these bugs can be very serious and can by symptomatic of significant design mismatches in the system.
- A bug is an indication of an error. If that error goes unseen and uncorrected then other code that relies on the error is built upon incorrect assumptions.
- Successful *Integration* is a prerequisite to successful *Functional Testing*.
- In the Agile community, *Integration* includes a fully working system—that is compiling, deploying, and testing— and not just a successful compile.

Therefore:

Instead of shying away from *Integration* because it is so painful and pushing it to the end of a release cycle—embrace the pain! Pain— in software development—means that something is not working well; we should use that feedback to fix the problem instead of ignoring it.

We traditionally think of *Integration* as something we "have to do" out of obligation—the only reason we are really doing it is to deliver the system to the client (a pretty important reason) and so we do so just before we are ready to release.

By reflecting on the pains of *Integration* we can get an idea of what values can be delivered by doing *Integration* well:

- Lack of *Integration* is a risk and masks several bugs. Therefore, by *integrating* more frequently we can discover the bugs early and often and perhaps avoid many compound-errors.

- The difficulty of *Integration* is almost always related to several manual steps and synchronization of different versions of code bases, libraries, and other resources to deliver a working product. There is nothing inherently un-automatable about these steps. Therefore spend the effort to automate all steps in *Integration*.
- *Integration* is a form of feedback and information regarding the global state of the system. If we want to be more "Agile" we always want feedback more frequently. Use this information as feedback for the entire team. Don't keep it hidden so that only those responsible for the build know what is happening.

Adoption:

The first step along the road to *Continuous Integration* is to automate your build. This means all manual processes must be removed[5]. Depending on your development environment there will be different tools to help you do this[6]. This may mean that you will have to change or augment your existing toolset if it does not support full automation (for example requires human interaction periodically with dialog boxes). This step can be done independently and does not need the full development team's involvement.

Once you have a fully automatic build you then need to get that build running regularly—preferably nightly—and produce a report that is available to the team. One of the best ways to do this is to put up an *Information Radiator*[7] that shows the build status. At this point the entire development team must be brought in and told that the build

---

[5] Some common processes are checking out the current code base for a build, tagging the files with a build number, generating the database schema, compiling the code, running automated tests, etc.

[6] In Java there are several open source projects such as Ant and Maven, in .NET there is NAnt and MSBuild, and there are several build tools (in addition to make) available in the C/C++ environment.

[7] An Information Radiator is an artifact that is placed within the development team's work area that is easy to read and understand—it "radiates" its information to those in its vicinity. Specifically a daily print-out, poster, or monitor to show the status of the build is needed.

status will be available daily and that fixing a build must become a priority.

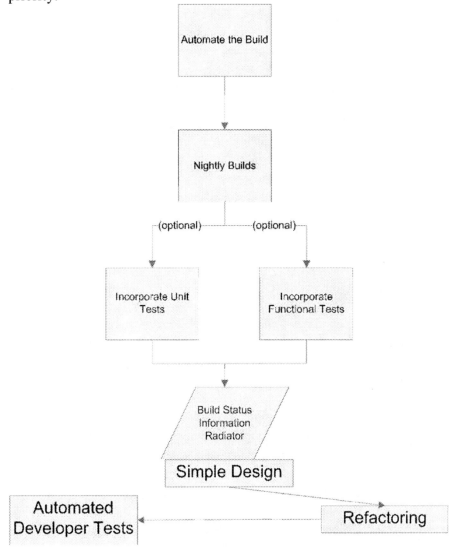

Figure 1 Steps in Adopting Continuous Integration

You want to get to the point where it is unacceptable for a build to be broken. It must be fixed before any new functionality is added to the code base. The next step towards achieving this point is getting your developers to the point where they can completely build the subsystem with a single script before they check in to avoid breaking the build. There are two parts to this step: 1) making the build script and the external deployment configuration available to developers locally on their desktop, and 2) making the build run fast enough so that developers can realistically test locally before checking in. Both of these steps have their challenges that, depending on your particular environment, may seem daunting. If this is a non-trivial problem for your team then set up one or more "deployment machines" where a developer can take the modified code and run a full build before checking the code in. Remember the human practices are more important than the tools. As a team you need to value *Integration* before check-in—especially during crunch time—to keep from breaking the build.

Once it is possible for developers to realistically perform a full *Integration* build before checking in we come to the heart of *Continuous Integration*—frequent feedback. Developers now have a tool that will let them integrate their new code into the entire system. How will they use it? How often? This new-found tool—full *Integration* on the developer's machine—should be used before each and every check-in to the source repository. Only upon a successful local *Integration* build should a developer check in code.

As a rule of thumb developers should integrate as often as possible to validate that their code works with the entire system. How often is that possible? This depends on how they develop software; practices like *Test-First Development* encourage a developer to build very small testable work; a developer using this practice may check in four or five times a day. Developers who are not already going that fast should strive to reach a daily check-in so that every day they force themselves to get to a point where they can integrate successfully[8].

---

[8] Many of us are used to taking a functional piece and working on it for several weeks and then checking it in (and waiting for *Integration* several months afterwards during the "hardening *Iterations*"). This is usually not because of any restrictions of the problem itself but rather our own way of working. Therefore strive to achieve a daily check-in as a minimum.

At that point every developer has at least daily feedback on the *Integration* state of the build. For the vast majority of check-ins the local *Integration* will go smoothly. A minority will break locally and the developer will be able to fix the problem before checking in the code. An even smaller minority may pass through the local build check and fail on the official build machine. At that point the team should identify which check-in caused the build to break, roll it back to get a successful build, and fix the problem offline. The local developer scripts should be modified to catch that new type of error that fell through the cracks.

Finally tests. We have intentionally not talked specifically about tests. *Continuous Integration*, as stated so far, without automated tests, is still extremely valuable. That said, if your team has *Automated Developer Tests* and/or *Functional Tests* then they should be incorporated into the *Continuous Integration* practice. They should be incorporated as early as possible, as part of or directly after automating the build process. At this point a definition of a broken build goes from one that doesn't compile or deploy to one that doesn't pass all of the automated tests.

But:

Continuous Integration sometimes becomes too slow or too brittle. If this happens then a major side effect is a continuously broken build. This is worse than useless. It acknowledges that something is wrong and does nothing about it. The development team becomes de-sensitized to the importance of the build process and it goes back to ugly step-child status again. Do what it takes to speed up the tests.

Frequent and long-lasting broken builds are the bane of *Continuous Integration*. As long as it is obvious who broke the build then there are usually no problems. How is it obvious who broke the build? If only one person, say Cindy Coder, checked code and the build broke ,then it is easy—Cindy is responsible.

But what if Cindy, Dave, Ashley, and Ahmed all checked in code. Then who broke the build? Often what happens is that they are all sure that they did not break the build and they have an "important task" that they cannot drop at this point in order to investigate the break. Anyway, they ran the build locally and nothing went wrong—it must be one of the others. Be warned: this is a very slippery slope. If the problem is not fixed, four more people will check in and possibly compound the problem. They ran their local builds and they all failed—but that is because of the earlier failure not *their* code, right? Your one test failure, if not fixed promptly, can easily turn to ten broken tests over a couple of days.

So what is the root problem here? The problem is that the build is too slow. If between one build and the next there are several people consistently checking in within one build cycle (rule of thumb is more than three) then the build needs to be faster. If you have a nightly build this is unavoidable. It can be mitigated by having one person—a Build Cop—be responsible for tracking down build failures and helping developers fix them. If you have true *Continuous Integration* then you must work to make your build faster. How to do this is extremely environment-dependent (sorry), so it really does depend. Be creative—remember builds are no longer the ugly stepchild and deserve your attention just as much as any other part of the development process.

Continuous Integration, especially during adoption, is not a free practice. For many development environments significant time will need to be invested to fully automate the build and bring its time down. Investment in time and effort from the entire development team in keeping the build running will be required.

Variations:

Continuous Integration is one of those practices that has caught on even in non-Agile shops because it keeps development environments running effectively and visible to management. Here are some common variations on *Continuous Integration:*

- *Continuous Integration* at an enterprise level. Each project has its own CI tool and the tools are linked hierarchically so that one build pulls only "successful" builds from the other.
- Single code repository: As *Automated Developer Tests* and *Functional Tests* are pulled into *Continuous Integration* (more detail in the *Test-driven Development* and *Test-driven Requirements* clusters) greater confidence in the quality of the code emerges. With this greater confidence the need for "branches" in the source code repository goes away. Teams start to have a single code repository that is *always* working.
- *Functional Testing* is more time consuming than *Automated Developer Tests* because it exercises the system as a whole. Some teams will pull these tests out of *Continuous Integration* and make them secondary. Because this is a common pattern it is important to call it out. It is equally important to point out that generally teams take this approach too early. By pulling these tests out of *Continuous Integration* you allow them to become stale and fail, thereby negating a very large portion of their benefit. If at all possible I recommend staying away from this solution by focusing on making your build and your tests run faster.

References:

There are several articles written and available on *Continuous Integration*. Any search engine will bring up several tools and articles. The original article, which was updated in May 2006, is:

Fowler, Martin. *Continuous Integration*.
http://www.martinfowler.com/articles/continuousIntegration.html

10

Simple Design

The complexity of your design should support the current requirements at hand and no more. By keeping designs simple, you can build your software more quickly, maintain it with less pain, and modify the design incrementally by relying on *Automated Developer Tests* and *Refactoring*.

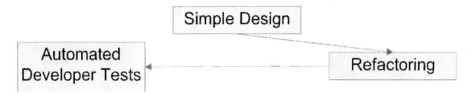

Business value:

Simple Design is a powerful practice that yields business value in reducing the time to market and cost of a software product because the team does not pay for what it does not need. It also increases a product's lifetime because a less complex design is easier to understand and has less inertia.

Sketch:

When Waterfall Will joined Scott the ScrumMaster's Agile Development team a year ago he had many misgivings about the project team and their coding techniques. Most importantly he had the burning question "Where is the Design?!" He could not fathom how starting with a Simple Design could ever work. In his experience a team must set the architecture and design upfront otherwise the frequent changes that will be required to change the design incrementally will incur exponential costs.

Will decided to suspend his disbelief for a few months and give this new development technique a chance. Grudgingly at first Will had to admit that the simple designs were elegant in their own way. As he observed again and again the resilience of these designs and how they could be easily changed according to new requirements because of the safety net of Automated Developer Tests he started to enjoy this way of development. His designs were much leaner overall and he recognized that this was not really getting rid of the design cycle but making design part of every day's work

Context:

You are on a development team that is building a software system with one or more of the following needs:

- Requirements change frequently so your system must be resilient to change.

- Your customer may not know exactly what he wants. You want to be able to give him something to work with as soon as possible to help him make a good decision.

- Your team wants to reduce time to market of your product significantly.

- Your team is working with complex or unfamiliar technologies and you want to leave major design decisions to the latest possible point when you have become more familiar with the problem and/or technologies.

Forces:

These are common problems typical to software development that are
addressed by this practice:

- Feedback between customers and developers is infrequent because
  of the large delay between requirements and working software.
- Functionality is very complex and developers have a tendency to
  "go off track" and come back to the customer with an incorrect
  solution.
- A significant portion of development in an over-designed
  application goes into understanding and using the abstractions built
  in—even if they are not used.
- Design complexity has a "Cost of Design Carry" that is paid every
  time a developer has to understand, use, or test the complex code.
  If this complexity is for "tomorrow" we still pay a cost today.
  Unfortunately tomorrow never comes for much of the complexity
  we developers build into our software.

Therefore:

In the Agile community we believe that building in complexity in
hopes of reducing the cost of change for the future is a false hope.
Generalizations provide much more flexibility than what is strictly
needed by the current requirements. In the Agile community, this type
of generalization is known, derogatively, as Big Design Up Front
(BDUF).

We are not fortune-tellers and cannot foresee all of the changes. The
upfront design is not for free—the extended generalizations made to
allow for change are more complex and harder to understand and
maintain than a Simple Design. The cost of carrying that design will
far outweigh the benefits gained.

The design should only be complex enough to meet the requirements
of the current *Iteration*. Your design should be a *Simple Design* that
has no generalizations for needs that will come in the future for two

reasons: (1) you really don't know what the requirements will be two years down the road and putting in those generalizations will incur a Cost of Design Carry over those two years, and (2) by enabling *Refactoring* via *Automated Developer Tests* you have reduced the cost of change and will be able to cost-effectively make the changes when new requirements dictate them.

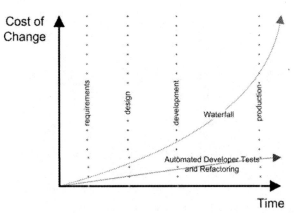

Figure 2 Cost of Change Curve for Waterfall and TDD

Adoption:

So how do you apply *Simple Design*?

1. Non-ambiguously determine what the requirements are for the task at hand.
2. Determine what the solution will look like. This can be done by writing the tests first and letting them drive the solution, or, more traditionally, by coming up with a design before starting to code.
3. If the solution uses existing code that is not general enough for the new requirements then *Refactor* the code to make it amenable to the addition of the new functionality. Rely on existing tests to verify that you have only changed design and not behavior.
4. Add the new functionality with a solution that is only as complex as needed to meet the new requirements.

Simple Design should not be practiced without the ability to refactor and evolve the design. *Refactoring*, in turn, cannot be done effectively without a set of *Automated Developer Tests*. These are the necessary practices for simple design.

To effectively adopt the practice of *Simple Design* most developers must suspend their disbelief[9] for several *Iteration*s in order to observe it working effectively.

But:

Watch out for these pitfalls:

- A team may drop *Simple Design* when some paths lead directly to where a BDUF would have led them. They see the constant *Refactoring* as a waste. They don't realize that most of the BDUF still leads to over-generalization; conversely most of *Simple Design* leads to less complex designs.
- A team may interpret *Simple Design* as the design that takes the least time. Frequently that includes cut and paste solutions. This is NOT *Simple Design*. This is bad code.
- Teams frequently do not adopt *Simple Design* because in their opinion, it cannot possibly work. It goes against all of their expertise and good sense. We highly recommend that teams suspend their disbelief as Waterfall Will did in the sketch of this pattern. Two to three months of practicing *Simple Design* regularly will make a believer out of a team!

Variations:

These are some common groupings of simple design with other practices. Both of the examples below are instances of the *Evolutionary Design* cluster.

---

[9] Most experienced developers have problems building a simple solution only for the requirements at hand. Years of generalizing and designing ahead for future flexibility makes most developers very hesitant to trust that design will be changeable without an exponential increase in effort later on.

- *Test-First Development, Simple Design, Refactoring.* Write the tests, build the simple design to pass the tests, and then refactor the simple design to make it more appropriate.
- *Simple Design, Test-Last Development, Refactoring.* Come up with a minimal design to meet the requirements at hand, develop the code based on that design, write the tests to exercise the code just written, and then refactor the design to better fit the (code) reality on the ground.

References:

Simple Design comes directly from eXtreme Programming:

Beck, Kent. 1999. *Extreme Programming Explained: Embrace Change.* Addison-Wesley Professional.
Beck, Kent and Cynthia Andres. 2004. *Extreme Programming Explained: Embrace Change. Vol. 2.* Addison-Wesley Professional.

11

(Automated) Functional Tests

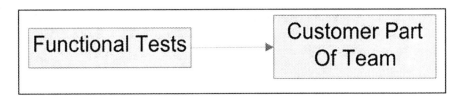

Business value:

Functional Tests primarily increase value to market and increase visibility of the software development team's progress by drastically improving the communication and validation of requirements. It also helps to increase product lifetime, reduce the time to market and reduce the overall cost of the system because it is a form of testing and feedback.

Sketch:

Mustapha Mentor has just joined Scott ScrumMaster's Agile team as a part-time consultant to help the team take the next step in improving their software development process. After two weeks on the team Mustapha noticed that a significant number of the User Stories were not passing approval by Chris Customer and Aparna Analyst. Upon further investigation Mustapha noticed that there were typically one or two days of "hardening" after a developer marked their tasks complete because of misunderstandings, mistakes, and omissions in the requirements-to-code translation.

Mustapha had seen this before. Although the team was practicing TDD, which helped them "solve the problem right," they still had minor problems in "solving the right problem." Iterations were forcing these mistakes to be caught and fixed regularly, but there was definite room for improvement.

Over the next several Iterations, Mustapha had the team read FIT for Development *by Rick Mugridge and Ward Cunningham and helped the team use the FIT tool to introduce a set of automated tests as requirements instead of User Stories. It was slow in Adoption, but after five or six Iterations of hard work and encouragement the team had reached a critical mass of tests and experience. The hardening period went away, development speed went up, and even the design quality improved!*

Context:

You are on a software development team and you want to significantly improve the quality of your software product. That is, you want to write code with less defects that sdoesn't just solve the problem right, but also solves the right problem! You and your team are also willing to put in a serious effort to gain this improvement. You are willing to revisit the existing design and architecture and change them to facilitate these improvements. You are also willing to slow down so that you eventually speed-up in performing these tasks.

Forces:

These are very common problems in software development that are addressed by this practice:

- Bugs increase as inter-module dependencies grow: Unit tests can keep individual classes fairly free of bugs, but they do not address inter-module bugs. Furthermore, as the code base grows, the number of potential inter-module bugs grows faster.

- Not knowing when a task is done: Almost everyone has experienced a project that was declared "done" and then continued for weeks or months afterward.
- Misunderstood requirements: Frequently, especially on distributed, international teams, traditional requirements are misunderstood because of cultural differences. What may be clear to one party is often very unclear to the other party.
- Imprecise requirements: One of the reasons projects drag on after they are declared "done" is that the original requirements were imprecise. Verbal and Prose requirements do not provide enough detail for coding. Developers guess what the customer meant and call the project done. But if the developers guessed wrong, the code will have to be re-worked.
- Contradictory requirements: Many "done" projects get stuck in the testing phase because of bug cycles. An example of a simple cycle is that when bug A is fixed, bug B appears; and when bug B is fixed, bug A re-appears. But the cycle is rarely that obvious, especially if A and B are in different parts of the system or take a long list of manual steps to reproduce.
- Outdated requirements: The longer running the project, the more likely that at least some of the requirements have fallen behind the code. Let us be frank—have any of us really had requirements that were 100% up-to-date after a year of development? Outdated requirements can be more nefarious than no requirements. If there are no requirements, developers will try to extract them from the customer, the code, or the unit tests, all of which are likely to provide fairly up-to-date information. But outdated requirements are *mis*-information. They can waste significant time by sending developers down the wrong track.
- Delayed releases: As the application grows and the product matures, the testing department cycle can take longer, causing increasingly delayed releases.
- Slow manual testing: Manual testing by a testing department will take significantly longer with a large product than a small one. Because manual testing is slow, the feedback about a bug occurs long after the code changes that caused the problem were made. The delayed feedback makes it hard to diagnose which change

caused the bug, so fixing a bug found by the testing department takes longer, too.

- Slow patches: A side effect of slow manual testing is slow patches for bugs reported in the field. In many development environments, developers have to set up a full database and perform many manual steps to reproduce a bug. And they must reproduce the bug both to diagnose it and to confirm they have eliminated it.

Therefore:

Introduce a form of *automated tests* that describe the business process to be coded up and treat them as "executable requirements." These executable requirements are written by the *Customer* at the beginning of each *Iteration* and provided to the developer(s). This is one of those practices that, unfortunately, is tool dependent. You will need a tool that is usable by non-programmers such as FIT(http://fit.c2.com/) or FITNesse(http://fitnesse.org/). The amount of precision required to write executable tests will require the *Customer* to be unambiguous and go to a level of detail that they may be unaccustomed to achieving so they may need help from either testers or developers. Define this type of tests as *Functional Tests*, that is business process tests that are co-owned by *Customers* and developers that can be automatically executed.

A *functional test* contains the information that a customer would normally use for acceptance testing after a developer has written the code. It is use case scenario with specific values entered. So, for example, let us assume that we have the requirements for an online grocery store application and the current requirements for this *Iteration* include getting the inventory management to work correctly. Here is an example FIT test that can be used as requirements. (Don't be intimidated by the table format—take some time to read the tables and consider them as requirements.)

Item Inventory Management Tests

Load Basic Data To Be Used For Tests

To start off with, let us load a standard set of items from an external source into our persistent store. Therefore our tests coming afterwards will have a non-trivial baseline of data.

fit.ActionFixture		
start	com.valtech.post.service.tests. fit.ItemInventoryFixture	
enter	inventory	./src/com/valtech/post/service/tests/fit/inventory.txt
check	total items	10

Ok, we have 10 items. Let's be sure we have the right details.

com.valtech.post.service.tests.fit.ItemInventoryDisplayFixture		
upc	description	price
2458	Chocolate	0.75
1234	Cola	0.99
9034	Toothpaste	2.34
3214	Milk	2.34
8743	Eggs	2.35
0987	Olives	2.43
1233	Apples	1.12
8745	Paper Towels	3.45
9457	Canned Soup	1.24
2345	Cheese	5.65

Now, with a successfully loaded set of items, let's do some catalog maintenance...

fit.ActionFixture		
start	com.valtech.post.service.tests.fit.ItemInventoryFixture	
enter	select	2458
check	description	Chocolate
enter	description	Dark Chocolate
check	description	Dark Chocolate
enter	add Item	1111
enter	description	honey
enter	price	5.60
check	total items	11

enter	remove Item	0987
enter	select	0987
check	upc	0987
check	description	Not Found
check	price	0.01

From a development standpoint, these tests should exercise the system from a layer just beneath the GUI. This is commonly known as the service layer or the system façade. Writing tests at this level exercise almost all of the system and all of the business logic (there should be no business logic in the GUI). Therefore *Functional Tests* ensure that the requirements have been met. Because the tests are written first they can be used by the developer to determine "doneness"—when the developer writes enough code so that test passes then the requirement has been met.

All of the executable requirements need to be written up as part of a test-suite that is run often—preferably as part of *Continuous Integration*. By consistently running the ever-growing test suite the system never breaks a requirement that has already been met without a test failing. This means that if any requirements contradict then at least one test will fail and the developer can go back to the *Customer* for clarification.

Upon successful adoption of *Functional Tests* you can expect the following benefits:

Development team has more confidence: There is a definite sense of confidence that developers acquire when there is a solid test framework that they rely upon. *Automated Developer Tests* and *Test-driven Development* go a long way in making developers more confident of their code. This is not merely a "warm-fuzzy" feeling (which is always good for morale), but enables faster development because developers change what needs to be changed via *Refactoring*. *Functional Tests* take this confidence up a notch or two above and beyond *Automated Developer Testing*. They also improve the confidence of the customers/analysts and testers because they have a direct relationship to the requirements and regression tests. They know a green test is a non-ambiguous indication that the related scenario is *working*.

Robust Tests: *Functional Tests* that drive the service layer instead of focus on business logic. Business logic tends to be fairly stable, and so the tests don't have to change much. In contrast, *automated tests* that hit GUI elements break when GUI elements are re-arranged.

Errors and bugs are reproducible quickly: Once a bug is found, a *Functional Test* is written, and that bug doesn't come back to haunt us. An *Automated Developer Test* should also be written around the buggy code, of course, but when developers first begin investigating a bug, they don't know where to write the *Automated Developer Test* because they don't know which unit caused the problem. But they (hopefully!) know which use case caused the problem, so they should be able to write a *Functional Test* immediately. By writing tests as soon as bugs are discovered, you eliminate the bug-fix-break thrashing that happens when systems become brittle.

When a system moves from initial development to production the amount of time spent developing new functionality decreases. With a *Functional Testing* framework at hand the "business language" has already been built and it becomes very straight-forward (more than for *Automated Developer Test*) to build a *Functional Test* that exactly reproduces the error based on the bug report. This allows the developer to have an executable reproduction of the bug that can be used for digging into the code repeatedly without having to keep setting up the environment "just so."

Testers Have Time to Be More Pro-Active: If slow manual testing is a force behind adopting *Functional Tests*, then quick automated testing is a benefit. The consequence is that testers are relieved of much of the day-to-day burden of manual testing of the main business rules. Instead, testers have more time to be pro-active, collaboratively helping developers design more testable code, rather than waiting to "clean up" at the end of an *Iteration*.

When a task is "done" is visible for all: Using *Functional Tests* does help us know when a task is done, but it's more than just that. *Functional Testing* makes progress visible to the entire development team—customer, analyst, developer, tester, and manager. At any point in time all passing (and failing) tests can be viewed. With a little effort business value produced at a functional level can be analyzed for management needs.

Better design, better architecture: *Functional Tests* drive better layer and subsystem separation. Consider the layers of a multi-tier architecture: since the *Functional Tests* execute through the service layer, every bit of business logic that has found its way into the presentation layer must either be duplicated in the test fixture or pulled into the service layer.

Similarly, consider the subsystems of the system—the modules with functional responsibility, such as a module for tax calculations. Any tax logic that has leaked out of the tax module will be duplicated in the test fixture unless it is moved into the tax module. *Functional Tests* help solidify the responsibilities of a subsystem.

Analysts think through requirements in greater detail: Analysts think through requirements in greater detail to achieve the descriptions needed to write a test. For example, an analyst might state that textboxes should be disabled whenever they are not needed. But when he writes a *Functional Test* for this requirement, he is forced to get explicit about which conditions cause which textboxes—or really their representations in the underlying service layer—to be disabled.

Improved customer-developer communication: Over time, the discussions of the *functional tests* help the team develop a common vocabulary and a common vision for the system (as Jim Shore shares his ideas http://www.jamesshore.com/Blog/A-Vision-For-Fit.html). Examples of the development of such collaboration can also be found in Mugridge and Cunningham's *Fit for Developing Software*.

Adoption:

So how does one go about adopting *Functional Tests* successfully as a practice?

1. Plan on testers/developers working with customers/analysts to write the tests together for the first few *Iterations*.
2. {Highly Recommended} Get some outside help: bring in someone who has successfully achieved *Functional Tests* within an Agile environment. This is much more than automated system level tests because they are an integral practice of development.
3. {Recommended} Pick up *Fit for Developing Software* and run a study group including customers, analysts, developers, and testers.
4. Choose a tool and don't build your own. FIT and Fitnesse are the most commonly used tools in this space.
5. Plan on your developer's building "fixtures" to support the "domain language" that the team will evolve. Do not try to short-circuit this by having customers and analysts learn the objects you've already built and the methods on them. This defeats the purpose of creating a Domain Language for your project.
6. Start with on analyst/customer and one developer for one story on one Iteration. Write the test as a use case scenario with explicit values.
7. Grow the team members who are aware of *Functional Tests* incrementally.
8. If you are working on an existing project then there is a good chance you will need to do some non-trivial *Refactoring* to accommodate tests. At this point you will need to have adopted *Automated Developer Tests* to enable *Refactoring*. If your team hasn't adopted these practices you will need to do so to move forward.
9. Do not put *Functional Testing* on hold but write the tests and use them manually until you can effectively *Refactor* the parts of the system needed for testing. Even if tests are not automated, this level of detail can be test-driven—that is the tests can be written down and used by developer's to determine "doneness."

10. During the transition to *functional tests*, it can help to assign a developer the role of "Functional Test Cop." The cop's job is to track down the developers who break the *functional tests*, help them see why their code broke the test, and help them fix the problem.
11. {Optional} Pick up *Domain Driven Design* and run a study-group after you have started to write *Functional Tests* successfully. Tie the language your team is coming up with directly to what is in this book.
12. Plan on a three to six months adoption period until your team starts to write *Functional Tests* regularly.
13. Plan on an adoption period anywhere from three to 12 months if this is already a long-running project without tests because you will probably need significant *Refactoring* efforts to enable this practice.

Like almost everything in Agile development, *Functional Tests* should be adopted iteratively. Be careful that you keep "people" ahead of "process." That is, iterate to get developers and customers trained and have them build a few *functional tests*. Then, after the team has a few working *functional tests* that are part of the build, ask them for feedback on the tools and processes. Improve your tools and processes until the developers and customers are happy with functional testing. Then iteratively expand the practice to the team.

But:

There are valid reasons that *Functional Tests* are not wide-spread in the Agile community. *Functional Tests* are very error prone. There are two general categories where things can go wrong. The first is in the adoption itself—and in that way this section is similar to all the other *But* sections for the other practices. The other significant area is that of the underlying system architecture. If the system architecture is not *Functional Test*-friendly then it needs to be changed.

Implementation Smells:

Little or no accountability for broken tests: If there is no accountability for broken tests, then they don't get fixed. In general there is no accountability if it is difficult to tell whose code change broke the test. This usually happens when the test-run cycle is significantly slower than the check-in cycle of developers; that is, if several developers have checked in their code since the last time the tests were run, it is difficult to determine whose changes broke the tests. So how do you address this problem? Simple. Make the tests run faster and here's how:

First, the team must make a commitment to functional testing as a primary development practice instead of a secondary one. When it is not an option to drop the tests, then teams find creative solutions. The main thing is to speed up the running of the *functional tests* so they can be run effectively by developers on their local machines before checking in. Effective strategies we have found are:

- *Functional Tests on Separate Machines:* By grouping tests into related suites then each suite can easily be run on its own machine. This effectively parallelizes the test suite and can give a speed increase proportional to the number of machines used.

- *Functional Tests Rollback Database Transaction:* This is a very simple but effective idea: don't commit your database transactions if you are testing end-to-end. We have seen this practice emerge independently on different projects and this usually gives about an order of magnitude increase in speed.

- *Functional Tests Refactored to Thinner Slices:* By testing a small scenario within each test instead of several scenarios (or even all scenarios) for a use case we get a finer granularity for splitting up tests. We have also found that larger tests tend to have more redundancy—breaking them up allows for faster individual tests.

- *Functional Tests Grouped By Business Area:* Grouping *functional tests* by business area allows a developer to test the subset of relevant tests on their machine without running the full suite. This allows for a faster red-green-red test loop and will keep a test suite from slowing the pace of development.

  Note that having independent database sandboxes for each functional test run is a prerequisite for the above advice. If two *functional tests* run against the same database, one may report an incorrect "failure" because of interactions with the data inserted by the other test.

- *Confidence in functional tests is lost:* Leaving tests broken takes away from much of the value of the *Functional Test* suite as a "safety net" that prevents bugs from entering the build in the first place. The tests aren't catching the bugs and helping us keep the code in working order as we would expect. Without this safety net, confidence in the tests is lost. Test writing is reduced, and in the more serious cases they are deleted and finally dropped as a whole.

- *Small code changes break many tests:* When many tests fail, one normally assumes that a big code change must have been checked in. However, if only a small change caused many failures, then there must be a large amount of overlap of the tests.

  To solve this have each test focus on a thin slice of functionality. When each test focuses on one thin slice of functionality and does not overlap much with other tests, then it's more likely that only one or two tests break when a bug is introduced. It is much easier to diagnose why a thin test failed. Thus, writing tests to exercise one thin slice of functionality in one major system provides the best feedback on that example of a business process.

- *Functional tests try—and fail—to catch unit level tests:* If functional testing does not reduce the bugs found by your testing group and customers, the problem may be that the bugs are at the wrong level for *Functional Tests*.

Functional Tests are not a replacement for *Automated Developer Tests*, even if the coverage statistics look high. *Automated Developer Tests* support *Functional Tests* by exercising the code most likely to break, even if it is deeply buried in otherwise inaccessible parts of the system under test. Use *Automated Developer Tests* for unit-level bugs and *Functional Tests* for interaction bugs.

- *Functional Tests are created without appropriate Refactoring*: Business logic is then copied into the fixtures used for the tool. Code duplication causes a maintenance nightmare. Don't do this. Tests are as important as production code. Do not introduce duplication; *Refactor* instead.

- *Feature Devotion sets in:* The feature list, tied to *Functional Tests*, becomes upfront requirements. Feedback is lost. You are now back in Waterfall Will's world!

- *Functional Tests used as a meter for progress.* This assumes that all functions are of equal value. They are not. You can easily fool yourself into thinking you are delivering business value because you've just delivered 40 running *Functional Tests*. What if these tests don't really have business value to your customer? Focus on business value.

Architecture Smells:

If you are using good tools and techniques and it's still hard to write *Functional Tests*, then the root problem may be your system's architecture. In particular, if your test fixtures contain business logic, rather than merely translating test specifications into method calls, then you will want to consider the smells below. We also consider a smell when it is hard for a functional test to run through a single, complete use case.

Functional Tests help push business logic into the correct layer (in a tiered architecture) and the correct functional module. When business logic has found its way into the wrong place, *Functional Tests* expose the misplacement.

- *Fixtures contain business logic that mirror GUI work*: If you find yourself writing fixtures that must perform business logic so that they mirror what is done in the GUI, you may have an architecture smell. A common cause of such duplicated business logic is the use of a canonical three-tiered architecture having presentation, domain, and persistence layers. Such architecture does not always succeed in keeping business logic away from the presentation layer. In fact, it is very common for GUIs in this setup to contain "control" logic.

  For example, a simple GUI to transfer money from one account to another (*account1, account2*) often does the following in the GUI:

  > *Account1.withdraw($100)*
  > *Account2.deposit($100)*

  This is simple logic, but it is *business* logic and not view logic. So, if your fixture for the *transfer(account1, account2)* function has this logic in it, then you have code duplication with the UI (which is bad), and you have uncovered business logic in the presentation layer (which is worse).

When you encounter this type of problem, the solution is to pull out the duplicate code in a common place. That place is the service layer, which lies between the presentation and domain layers and contains control logic. In this way, *functional tests* help in proper separation of business and presentation logic and encourage a new logical layer to hold control logic.

- *Fixture for a module contains business logic that belongs in the module:* There is another way that business logic can turn up in a test fixture—when a functional module fails to contain all the business logic that belongs in it. An example can best illustrate this point.

Let us assume that one of our subsystems is a tax module that is responsible for doing all tax-related calculations. Before introducing functional testing, we wrote this module and believed we had good functional separation. Unfortunately, over the development of our project not everyone using the tax module was completely familiar with it, so some "pre-calculation" was made outside of the tax module depending on special tax-exempt days. This functionality should have been in the tax module; in a sense, the tax module's boundary was breached.

When *functional tests* were written for the tax module, we would find that the fixture code had to perform the "pre-calculation" that depended on the tax-exempt days. At that point, a responsible developer would notice the duplication and refactor the calculation into the tax module and out of the fixture and the non-tax-module code.

Functional Tests frequently solidify the boundaries and responsibilities of the subsystems. *Functional Tests* help focus your system's modules.

Functional Tests are difficult to run through a single, complete use case: Legacy systems—that is, systems that were not designed with functional testing—can be especially difficult to test. Sometimes they do not let you easily run through a single example of a business process. This is a very difficult smell to eradicate, and the solution depends on the architecture.

In some cases, the source of the problem is that a module assumes that multiple use cases are run simultaneously. When you try to isolate a single use case, you discover you still have to perform the set up for all the other use cases or the system crashes.

Variations:

Here are several different variations for using *Functional Testing* effectively

Covering the domain only: The adoption section focuses on *functional tests* that execute logic from the service layer through the domain layer all the way down to persistence. Not all *functional tests* must exercise all these layers; in fact Mugridge and Cunningham in *Fit for Developing Software,* argue for writing *functional tests* to exercise the domain logic only. Such tests are still useful, but they do not cover the subsystem boundaries, which are bug-prone. The domain-only approach is a viable alternative if running end-to-end tests within a developer-check-in cycle is infeasible.

Functional tests written by committee: Customers or analysts should write *functional tests* because they are in the best position to write requirements. However, testers and developers can join customers and analysts to co-write tests.

Testers bring their expertise in test-case development and help write requirements that cover the necessary details. Developers may be needed to help make the requirements executable depending on the tool. For example, the Framework for Integrated Tests (FIT) tool requires developers to write fixtures before tests can execute. Writing tests by committee usually happens primarily in the beginning stages of adoption of functional testing as analysts learn to think like a tester, and developers build their domain language. In later stages, writing tests by committee tapers off and the brunt of test authoring falls to the analysts with occasional help from others in the development group.

Functional tests are written with unit testing tool: Some teams write their *functional tests* with a unit testing tool such as NUnit or JUnit.

Using an xUnit testing tool covers code adequately but loses involvement from customers and analysts, since the tests are now coded in a language that they can neither write nor read. It becomes the developer's job to translate the requirements into these tests. The status of the tests as passing or failing is also not visible to either the customer or testing group.

Depending on who writes the tests they could be a valid variation or a smell. If the *Customer* is technical and writing the tests then this is a valid variation. Otherwise, if the *Customer* is somehow telling the developer and then the developer is translating that into code, then *functional tests* in xUnit tend to be rather hobbled because of the exclusive focus on coverage. These tests are indeed better than no *functional tests* but could be considered a smell.

Functional tests within a traditional development environment: So far, documented experience with functional testing is within an Agile development environment, but there is no reason it cannot be used on non-Agile projects. The key point is that the *functional tests* must be run at a frequency that matches the developer check-in cycle. That way, the source of failing tests can be identified. All of the benefits of Agile functional testing are achieved, just at a slower cycle time because there is no continuous *Integration* build. When done in this environment, the emphasis on speed of running tests is reduced because the check-in cycles are typically much longer.

References:

Functional Tests, as defined here, is most commonly discussed within the context of FIT, the Framework for Integrated Tests:

Gandhi, P., N. Haugen, M. Hill, and R. Watt. 2005. "Creating a Living Specification Document with FIT." http://www.Agile2005.org/XR22.pdf.

Marick, Brian. 2002. Bypassing the GUI. *Software Testing and Quality Engineering* September / October 41–47.

Mugridge, R., and W. Cunningham. 2005. *FIT for Developing Software: Framework for Integrated Tests.* Upper Saddle River, NJ: Pearson Education.

Shore, Jim. "A Vision For Fit." http://www.jamesshore.com/Blog/A-Vision-For-Fit.html.

12

Collective Code Ownership

**Members of the development team have the right and
responsibility to modify any part of the code.**

Business value:

Collective Code Ownership is a supporting practice for many other
Agile practices. Nonetheless, it does have a direct affect on increasing
the flexibility of your project by increasing the knowledge and
responsibility of software developers on a team to create a full solution
as opposed to a band-aid.

Sketch:

Scott ScrumMaster's team had read about Collective Code Ownership
in Extreme Programming Explained *by Kent Beck but decided not to
adopt it. In fact they felt it would be wasteful and counter-productive
to have anyone write GUI code, for example, because they would get
some really poorUIs from non-experts. Or so they thought...*

*Scott's team started with Iterations and Automated Developer Tests.
They quickly found that the old way of distributing work led to a
consistent block at the end of each Iteration for Integration work
between the different subsets of the code being done.*

*After a two Iterations of several missed goals they decided to give
Collective Code Ownership a try. This led to several spurious*

instances of Pair Programming throughout the Iteration for knowledge transfer between the team members. This also led to the goals being met much more easily and reduced bottlenecked resources.

Context:

You are on a development team that has traditionally specialized developers. Examples of this type of specialization are GUI developers, middle tier developers, and database developers. Developers on your team own the code they write and zealously protect it: "nobody touches *my code!*."

Your team is adopting one or more Agile practices that are moving you away from static designs created upfront to a more fluid design. Your team members have a need to modify more than their traditional piece of code to keep the system working.

Or you want to reduce the resource bottlenecks in your team—you don't want a single point of failure in your team's expertise. You want to be able to roll people on and off the team over time.

Forces:

There are many forces that emerge from adopting other Agile practices that are addressed by *Collective Code Ownership:*

Any form of change to the system can potentially cause other parts of the system to change. Many Agile development practices enable and encourage change. In fact, the subtitle of Extreme Programming Explained was "Embrace Change" which was one of the early mantras of the Agile community.

- To keep *Automated Developer Tests* passing for the entire system, developers will need to periodically modify parts of the system they did not write.

- *Refactoring* frequently causes the same issue: the need to modify parts of the system that you did not write because they depend on the part of the code you have.
- *Evolutionary Design* is severely limited if you cannot change parts of the system you did not write.
- *Continuous Integration* forces the entire system to be running and integrating all of the time. Therefore changes that affect multiple parts of the system must be fully resolved before that code is committed to the source repository.

Therefore:

To enable the agility of many Agile practices developers must be empowered to change any part of the system as needed. This should not be attempted without a safety net of tests—via *Automated Developer Tests*—to support developers in unfamiliar territory. The code becomes communal and mutually owned by the team. When a task requires a change in one part of the system that propagates to another part of the system, a developer should be encouraged to make the entire change or seek out help for that change if needed. This practice, of everyone owning the code and being allowed and encouraged to change it when needed, is called *Collective Code Ownership*.

Adoption:

You will find that *Collective Code Ownership* is pulled by many other practices for support. So don't consider adopting this practice until another practice creates a need for it. Once there is a need for *Collective Code Ownership* then:

1. Decide the scope of the communal code. This will often be the entire system. Sometimes it is the subsystem that your team is concerned with if you are one of many teams working on the same software product.

2. {Highly Recommended} Consider adopting *Automated Developer Tests* as a safety net to help ease the pains as developers become familiar with new parts of the system.
3. Set a rule that *developer A* cannot refuse to help *developer B* if *developer B* needs help on a part of the system that *developer A* is an expert in. That way *developer B* can make safe changes to parts of the code he is not familiar with yet.
4. {Highly Recommended} Adopt *Pair Programming* to share the knowledge of different parts of the system. Rotate pairs frequently.
5. Encourage developers to sign up for development tasks in different parts of the system, even if they are not familiar with those parts. This will also help spread the expertise across the team.

But:

This is another one of those non-intuitive practices that experienced developers have a hard time buying into. In fact, it is a little threatening to someone who feels a sense of security in being "the expert" in a particular part of the system.

- Developer's cannot let go of the "my code" mentality and become protective/defensive/aggressive when someone changes code that they originally wrote. These are growing-pains and should be dealt with on an individual basis.
- Designs "thrash" because developers are not communicating and/or respecting each other's decisions. Developers should only change existing designs in response to requirements driving those changes. Frequently you will find that one of the developers is changing the design "back to the right way" out of the my-code mentality instead of writing code to meet specific requirements.

Variations:

On large teams it may not be feasible to have generalists on the team because of the many different technologies that must be learned. One way to address this is to move from generalists to multi-part specialists. Developers learn the technologies and code of the neighboring subsystems of the one they are mainly focused upon.

References:

Collective Code Ownership was one of the original 12 practices of eXtreme Programming.

Beck, Kent. 1999. *Extreme Programming Explained: Embrace Change*. Addison-Wesley Professional.

Beck, Kent and Cynthia Andres. 2004. *Extreme Programming Explained: Embrace Change vol. 2*. Addison-Wesley Professional.

Part 3:

The Clusters

13

Clusters of Practices

Extreme Programming (XP) is one of the best known Agile development processes. In 1999 *Extreme Programming Explained* by Kent Beck outlined 12 practices that were to be practiced together — all 12 of them. These practices were to be used together to support each other and you were not to drop or modify any of them. These practices were "generative practices"—that is the value delivered by the whole was much greater than the sum of the individual parts. These practices had a synergy and when they were all used together wonders happened.

Kent Beck never said "thou shalt do all 12 practices," but in the early days that was definitely the mantra in the community. That is until Kent came out with *Test-driven Development* which was a subset of the 12 practices that was focused only on the programming practices of an individual developer.

The fact is that there are practices that have a synergy with each other such that you get an extra bang for your buck when you practice them together. These practices are what we call "generative" practices. There are also practices that are dependent on one another—for example, you cannot really *Refactor* without *Automated Developer Tests*—but don't confuse dependencies for generativity. They are different concepts.

This brings us to the third part of the book—the clusters. Clusters are groups of generative practices. Clusters are more than just the collection of practices; they also have an overall focus. So use these clusters to decide which practice to augment to your growing set of Agile practices. This doesn't mean that clusters should be your drivers —business values and smells should still drive your *Adoption* strategy — but clusters can help you get to the next level.

The clusters in this part of the book are also in pattern format just like the practices. Therefore they have their own *Adoption* section that will guide you towards an iterative *Adoption* of its constituent practices.

This final part of the book contains three of the most common clusters of practices with respect to the technical group of patterns I've covered so far in this book. There are many more Agile practices and there are many more clusters of generative practices out there. If you are interested in other clusters of practices then check the Agile practice adoption wiki (www.Agilepracticepatterns.org) periodically because this is an on-going pattern-mining process.

14

Evolutionary Design

To have a truly iterative development process[10] the design of the system must evolve as new requirements are built out. This is achieved by starting off with a *Simple Design* and changing that design only when the requirements force that change. The mechanics of changing a design is called *Refactoring* and is enabled by a form of *Automated Developer Tests*.

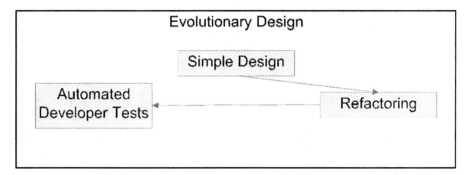

Business value:

Evolutionary Design, like its main practice *Simple Design*, reduces time to market and the cost of the software product. The synergy between the practices and focus on changing the design as needed accelerate these values more than the individual practices and also increases the flexibility of a product. Furthermore, *Evolutionary Design* also increases the product's lifetime.

---

[10]And not just a waterfall process with time-slices.

Sketch:

Amy Architect was part of Scott ScrumMaster's initial Agile project. She was a hands-on architect who frequently coded with developers on her team. She knew there was no "Architect" role on Scott's team and looked forward to the challenge. The rest of the team was glad to have her join them because of her experience and talent in building software.

Because they knew they were going to move fast they decided to perform Iterations and to practice Simple Design. Of course they also knew that to effectively be able to change the Simple Design later, they would need Automated Developer Tests, so they started with Test-Last Development because Test-First Development was too alien.

This was the team's first Agile project so they, out of habit, deferred to Amy in design decisions and came to her often for advice. She was more than happy to help, but she had a habit of going to a generalized design to allow for flexibility (as many of us do). The result was that the designs were very elegant and too complex for the requirements at hand. After a few Iterations Amy was pairing with Jim Jr. Developer and she was trying to explain how the particular design used the "Template Method design pattern" to allow for a family of algorithms. Jim didn't really get it, so to show him she took away the abstraction and inlined the solution. "Oh! I get it. So we did this template method thing for the future? But I thought we were doing Simple Design." They took out the complex design and put in the more simple and direct solution. The tests continued to pass because they had changed the design and preserved the behavior (i.e. Refactored the code).

That got Amy thinking about how much time was devoted to dealing with complex designs. She noted how easy it had been to make the change from the complex to the simple design and how the tests had given her confidence that the system still worked. So she started to remove complexity whenever she was pairing and they encountered code that was over-abstracted. After a few more Iterations the design became leaner and to her surprise it had complexity in different places than she would have guessed initially.

The software development team still came to Amy for advice in design but the advice she gave differed. She would always give the most obvious solution and only suggested generalized solutions when they were mandated by the requirements at hand. Over the months she watched the synergy between Automated Developer Tests, Simple Design, and Refactoring result in a lean and elegant system that was much more maintainable than anything she would have come up with at the outset. Her experience was still very valuable and needed by the team but it was more of a guiding hand rather than a dictator.

Context:

You are on a development project. That's it because this is one of those things that is applicable to all types of development projects. The next points in the context are a more "obvious fit" but are not necessary.

You are on a development project where time to market is very important.

Or you are on a development project that uses technologies that are new to a large part of the team. (eg. an ATG-Dynamo group starting to its first JEE Project is experienced in building web applications but is new to java and JEE.).

Forces:

These are problems that are found with almost all traditional development processes because they primarily stem from upfront design:

- The traditional practice of "design upfront" is based on the assumption that the cost of change is exponential with time. Disciplined practice of *Automated Developer Tests* and

Refactoring reduces the cost of change so that it is possible to change design in the development cycle.

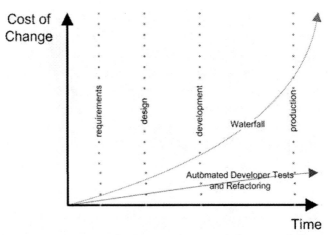

*Figure 3 Cost of Change Curve with Waterfall
and Evolutionary Design*

- The cost of upfront design involves much more than just a design diagram:
  - o The requirements and specifications must be detailed enough to support the design decisions.
  - o The design itself must be created and communicated to the team building the software.
  - o Software that is complex enough to implement the design must be created.
  - o The *Cost of Design Carry* for the extra generalizations that may or may not be used regularly accumulates every single day for every developer. Each task they perform is complicated because the developer must understand and use the framework built out to satisfy the upfront design.
  - o The software built on top of the upfront design implementation is more error prone because of its complexity.
- Software problems are generally complex and not straightforward. Knowledge is a team's most powerful tool for building software. Knowledge is attained through building the system. You will make a better design decision tomorrow after experience on the

project than you can make today because through the actions taken in building the system you and your team will learn.

Therefore:

Do not do *any* upfront design. No matter how much experience you have don't look forward. Constantly reinvent. Use *Automated Developer Tests* to enable your team to change the design of your system on an as-needed basis. Start with *Simple Design* and only *Refactor* that design when a requirement currently being built needs it. Trust that the tests you have built will warn you if you break anything during a *Refactoring* from one design to another. Do not patch or band-aid your system—if a requirement makes a design unsuitable then change it.

By using the three practices together, *Automated Developer Tests, Simple Design,* and *Refactoring* you will:
* Deliver faster because you always have the simplest design for the given requirements.
* Capitalize on your learning throughout the project to make better design decisions later. This will produce a design for your system that is much leaner than one created upfront. Because you have a leaner design, your maintenance cost will go down because the design is easier to understand (*Simple Design*) and easier to modify because of the *Automated Developer Tests.*
* Handle more complex problems successfully because you don't have to deal with all of the complexity at once.

Adoption:

Adoption of the *Evolutionary Design* cluster follows directly from the adoption of *Simple Design* because it requires *Refactoring* which, in turn, requires *Automated Developer Tests.* So:

1. Determine which type of testing you will adopt by reading patterns for *Automated Developer Tests, Test-Last Development,* and *Test First Development.*

2. Adopt *Simple Design* concurrently with *Automated Developer Tests*.
3. {Highly Recommended} Consider *Pair Programming* as a helpful practice during adoption of these practices. It helps to have a partner to keep you from slipping when adopting such disciplined practices.
4. Read and prepare for *Refactoring* as indicated in that pattern and begin to change your designs when your requirements force you to modify your designs.

At this point you have successfully adopted all three practices. Now you need to focus on the quality of each of these practices. Is the team really coming up with *Simple Designs* or are they following in the steps of Amy Architect in the sketch and over-designing? Is *Refactoring* being considered before and after every single task? If not then although all of your practices are present, they are not feeding into each other to cause your design to evolve. Here are some steps you should take until you are satisfied that you are indeed evolving your design:

5. Have a weekly brown-bag design review. Have one developer present some code that he has worked on.
   a. Critique the design from the point of view of *Simple Design*.
   b. If it is overly complex then make suggestions on how this can be done differently.
   c. Try to get down to the reasons why it is not an appropriate level of complexity. Is the reason too much upfront design? Is it failure to *Refactor* before and after a task when needed?

6. Watch out for significant bugs that fall through *Automated Developer Tests* to QA. If large problems arise from *Refactoring,* such as introducing bugs that are not caught, then your *Automated Developer Tests* are not enough.

But:

Evolutionary Design is not hacking. It is a very disciplined and constant implementation of the three practices in this cluster. Teams frequently loosen up on one of the practices to the detriment of the other two because of their synergistic relationship. These are the most common break-downs of individual practices:

- Poor *Automated Developer Tests* will directly affect the team's ability to *Refactor*. Design is changed to meet new requirements, all of the tests pass, it is checked in and all Hell breaks loose. Failing to build a good safety net of tests causes the cost of change to skyrocket because now all of the old headaches about finding the bugs, fixing it, and having others build on faulty code come back.
- Infrequent *Refactoring* means that developers are forcing requirements onto a design that does not smoothly support them. The lack of *Refactoring* means that you will have several band-aid solutions and the cost of change goes back up because the code is now harder to understand and use correctly. Eventually you will hit a brick wall because you started with *Simple Design* and have not evolved the design. At that point you will have one or more large *Refactorings* which are significantly more difficult to address.

Evolutionary Design can lead to a non-consistent architecture as each group evolves their own solution for similar problems. There are several ways that teams have addressed this particular problem:

- Have an architect of the team be the keeper of the "theory of the code." In this role, the architect keeps abreast of the evolving designs by reading code, pairing with different developers, running ad-hoc design reviews, etc. She then cross-pollinates the information and guides the solutions towards a cohesive set—the theory of the code.
- Build the architecture out with a smaller team where it is easy to have a cohesive design/architecture evolve. Have this initial team

build broad so they build a little of everything and solve the hard problems. At this point grow the team. This is explained in greater detail in <u>Divide After You Conquer.</u>

• Have an architect play a more central role so that all major design decisions go through her.

Variations:

As indicated in the *But* section, one of the problems of *Evolutionary Design* with large projects is inconsistency of design across the team. A technique called <u>Divide After You Conquer</u> is frequently used to mitigate this problem by starting every large project with a small core team that builds out a thin layer of the entire application. This allows the architecture to evolve to meet real requirements. And, because it is a small team, consistency is not a problem.

References:

Evolutionary design is not explicitly called out in the major process books but it is frequently discussed with *Simple Design*. The references therefore are the same as those in *Simple Design*:

Beck, Kent, *Extreme Programming Explained: Embrace Change*, Addison-Wesley Professional, 1999.

Beck, Kent and Andres, Cynthia, *Extreme Programming Explained: Embrace Change v2*, Addison-Wesley Professional, 2004.

15

Test-driven Development

Test-driven Development is a very effective cluster of practices that brings *Automated Developer Tests* to the forefront of development and suborns the design to testability. This form of development produces very loosely coupled designs that are (relatively) easy to evolve as requirements change.

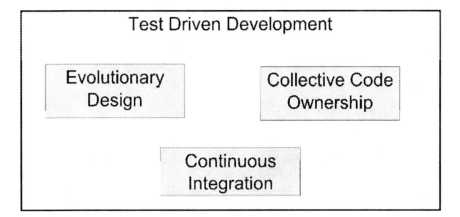

Business value:

Test-driven Development encompasses almost all of the practices in this book. It also, because of the generative nature of clusters, accelerates the business values of the practices. Most notably, *Test-driven Developmen*, increases quality to market, time to market, and product lifetime significantly. It also increases flexibility and reduces the cost of development just like *Evolutionary Design.*

Sketch:

Cindy Coder, Dave Developer, Waterfall Will, Uthman Upfront Design, Amy Architect, and Jim Jr. Developer are the developers on Scott ScrumMaster's team. They are practicing Test-driven Development, and although they did not really set out to be doing the full set of practices, one practice led to another.

Their team started with Automated Developer Tests because this was the most obvious win. Some developers ended up doing Test-First Development and others were more comfortable with Test-Last Development. Collective Code Ownership was quickly pulled in by this type of development to keep all of the tests running all of the time. Simple Design came in later, it was not that obvious a practice to the more experienced developers who couldn't really fathom not doing a design upfront. But, as the tests started to accumulate and Refactoring became a reality, Simple Design became attractive. After a several Iterations of Simple Design the design of the entire system slowly started to evolve and become very lean. The set of practices they had adopted had a synergy that made them much more valuable—not only were they developing better code but the entire system was becoming leaner. None of the team had seen this before on their non-Agile teams—systems always became worse because of entropy.

The team did not always have a Continuous Integration build running because it took a while for Bob BuildMaster to get the project building fast enough for this practice. They did, however, always run all of the tests locally before checking in code. When Bob approached them with his plans they gave him their full support. After the addition of this tool, and the ability to run a full integration locally on their machines, the development process took another notch up in speed and quality.

Context:

You are on a development team that wants to significantly improve its productivity. You want to build the software faster, with fewer bugs, be able to change the design as requirements change, and reduce the overall cost of the software over its lifetime.

You are aware that to have such a transformational change in your results will require a significant change in the way you build software. You and your team are willing to spend anywhere between three months to a year learning these skills. You are willing to make an investment by requiring less from your development team until these skills take hold.

Forces:

Test-driven Development is a cluster of several practices and therefore all of the forces of its building blocks—*Evolutionary Design, Continuous Integration, Collective Code Ownership*—are valid here. That is, *Test-driven Development* will ultimately resolve all of those forces. But what are the forces that would encourage a team to adopt the full set of practices within *Test-driven Development* instead of any of its subsets?

- *Evolutionary Design* builds software with minimal design as its focus. This technique uses testing as a tool to allow the design to evolve via *Refactoring*. The testing is not the driving factor behind the design.
- If testing is not at the heart of the software process then tests may or may not adequately exercise the system.
- Testing is a sampling process. It is infeasible to execute the entire state-space of all but the most trivial of programs. Therefore tests must be written with care to make sure that every test counts.
- Tests, at their best, are a form of executable requirements.
- Some *Refactorings* lead to changes that ripple across the system. For a significant change to be made while maintaining 100% passing tests, these subsystem effects must be addressed.
- A "successful build" should include all of the possible tests available on the system.
- To continuously improve software Agile practices focus on frequent feedback. There are several successful "rhythms."

Continuous Integration is a hook for running the tests on a "build machine."

- In a team environment *Evolutionary Design* can cause challenges as team members make significant changes to the design over time—there is no "upfront" design spec to be adhered to. A communication void is created by removing the upfront design that is not completely filled with *Evolutionary Design*. A team must effectively communicate the knowledge of the current design since it is no longer static.

Therefore:

To get a significant improvement in time to market, quality to market, flexibility, and a cost reduction in a team environment consider adopting *Evolutionary Design, Continuous Integration*, and *Collective Code Ownership*. Each of these practices are described as individual patterns elsewhere in this book.

Make testing a primary focus of your development effort:

Make all tests part of *Continuous Integration*. Change the definition of a successful build to include passing of all *Automated Developer Tests*.

Increase your *Refactoring* ability and speed by introducing *Collective Code Ownership*. Allow and encourage developers to make the changes necessary to make all tests pass even if they are in different subsystems.

Focus *Evolutionary Design* on tests more than design. Let the tests drive the development. The design will stay simple and will continue to evolve but will be driven solely by tests. By doing this you will make sure not to write a line of production code without tests. This focus will push your designs to be even more loosely coupled which, in turn, will increase the lifetime and flexibility of your system.

Upon successful adoption of these practices and cluster with a focus on tests you will have a team that is delivering software of much higher quality and flexibility at an increased pace for less money. But remember, this hinges on discipline with all of the practices and time to learn this new form of development.

Adoption:

There are two popular forms of *Test-driven Development* that differ by the type of *Automated Developer Tests* done. *Test-First* development is superior to *Test-Last* but harder to adopt successfully.

1. Plan for a lengthy period before you get to the point where the different practices are working effectively enough for the generative nature of this pattern to kick in. For small teams on a green field project this may take three months and for large teams with an existing code base without any tests it may take up to a year to see full benefit.
2. Have trust in your development team. Trust them to make the changes necessary. Give them the space to learn. Create an environment that rewards the practices you want them to adopt.[11]
3. Start with the adoption of *Evolutionary Design* as a team. At the same time spawn off an effort to adopt *Continuous Integration*.
4. {Highly Recommended} Introduce *Pair Programming* as a helpful practice to adopt *Evolutionary Design* and its constituent practices. *Pair Programming* will help with the discipline of always writing tests because it is easier to be lazy when you are coding alone. It also gives a natural vehicle for *Collective Code Ownership* to spread expertise across the team. Use this as an adoption tool. You are free to continue pairing or drop the practice upon successful adoption.
5. When *Evolutionary Design* leads to *Refactorings* that break the tests for more than the code being written, pull in *Collective Code Ownership*.

---

[11] This is a little touchy-feely, but it is really one of the most successful adoption strategies for any practice. How do you create an environment so that your team wants to adopt the practices?

6. *Continuous Integration* will generally be available before the team is completely comfortable with writing *Automated Developer Tests* in a disciplined fashion. At that point introduce the notion, tools, and practice to the full team as described in the *Continuous Integration* pattern.
7. When you feel the team has become comfortable with *Evolutionary Design, Continuous Integration,* and *Collective Code Ownership*, then step back and examine your process. Focus the practices around testing even more:
   o If you are using *Test-Last Development* consider moving to *Test-First Development* instead. Otherwise augment the practice with periodic code reviews of tests.
   o Make sure that the tests drive your design and not the other way around where your design determines the tests. This is one of the main drivers of loosely coupled designs emerging using these practices.
   o Can you read the tests for existing code as a form of documentation? A hallmark of good *Test-driven Development* is tests that can be read as documentation of the production code.

But:

Test-driven Development is a collection of practices that delivers significant value to the customer. It is dependent on everyone on the team doing their part in continually and diligently writing tests, evolving the design, keeping the build running, and working with each other to fix broken tests caused by some *Refactorings*. The problem comes down to this: if any one practice is allowed to slip then the generative nature of this cluster will be lost. Here's what can happen if one of the practices is not done diligently:

• If *Collective Code Ownership* is dropped then this will severely limit successful *Evolutionary Design* because the tests broken by a significant design change will not be fixed in a timely manner.
   o This may lead to code check-in with broken tests. This is the greatest of all evils (or at least one of the really big ones) in

Test-driven Development. This leads to the breakdown of 100% passing tests and a breakdown of *Continuous Integration* that includes the tests.

o It may lead to the code not being checked in and handed over to the person who can fix the tests. This slows down development speed and bottlenecks the person who has the knowledge to fix the broken tests.

- If *Evolutionary Design* breaks down or any of its component practices then you have just lost at least 50% of the effectiveness of *Test-driven Development.* See the *Evolutionary Design* cluster for details on keeping it running well.

- If *Continuous Integration* breaks down then you lose the ability to quickly know that your code changes are good within the entire system. *Evolutionary Design* will continue to function but at a slower pace.

- *Collective Code Ownership* may not be enough to enable fixing of broken tests in an unfamiliar part of the code due to *Refactoring.* Even if the developer is encouraged to change the code, they may not have the expertise to do so. Introduce *Pair Programming* to allow the sharing of knowledge.

- What you are doing with *Test-driven Development* is building better software. Whether that software actually addresses the customer's needs is not addressed by this cluster. Do not get a false sense of security that you are building more *valuable* software to the client. Look to other practices such as *Functional Testing, Test-driven Requirements,* and *Customer Part of Team* to help you build software that is valuable to the customer.

Variations:

TDD enables single source repository: Consider going to a single source code repository instead of branches for each release, patch, etc. This will be enabled by this cluster because you will always have a working code base that integrates and passes all developer tests. By going to a single source repository you will free up a significant amount of time to be used elsewhere.

References:

There are several references for Test-Driven Development. Here are a few:

Astels, David, 2003. *Test-Driven Development: A Practical Guide*, Upper Saddle River, NJ: Prentice Hall.

Beck, Kent. 2003. *Test-Driven Development By Example*. Boston, MA: Pearson Education.

Feathers, Michael. 2005. *Working Effectively with Legacy Code*. Upper Saddle River, NJ: Prentice Hall.

Jeffries, Ron. 2004. *Extreme Programming Adventures in C#*. Redmond, WA: Microsoft Press.

Martin, Robert C. 2003. *Agile Software Development: Principles, Patterns, and Practices*. Upper Saddle River, NJ: Pearson Education,

16

Test-driven Requirements

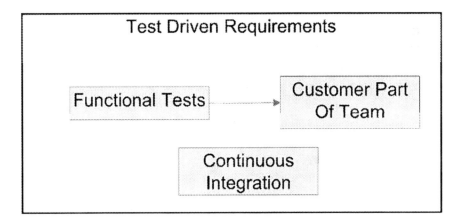

Business value:

Test-driven Requirements delivers enhanced value to market and increases the visibility of the project's progress significantly by creating a tight loop of communication and feedback between the customer and the development team. By combining *Functional Tests* and *Continuous Integration* the feedback is greatly enhanced. *Test-driven Requirements* also addresses all of the other business values as a form of system testing, therefore the time to market is reduced, the product lifetime increases, the quality to market increases, the flexibility of the entire application is enhanced, and the total cost of the software system is reduced. *Test-driven Requirements* is a truly valuable cluster of practices that is frequently undervalued.

Sketch:

Aparna Analyst, Tina Tester, and Cindy Coder have been practicing Agile development—specifically Iterations and Test-driven Development, with Simple Design and Continuous Integration—for six months and have become adept at the practices. They have significantly increased their rate of development and significantly reduced the bug count. It is not, however, zero and there is still room for improvement. At the last Retrospective they recognized this as a place for improvement.

They decided that what's good for the goose is good for the gander: if TDD helped developers then taking it a step further and writing executable, then automated tests for the requirements at the beginning of each Iteration will help the entire team. They realized that it would not all be the developers' responsibility as in TDD but it would really involve the entire team. Aparna, Tina, and Cindy volunteered to try this out with Caleb the Consultant as their guide and mentor.

The team is currently nearing the end of the first Iteration where they tried this set of practices and Aparna's head hurts from having to document the requirements so specifically. Tina is pleasantly surprised—these tests look exactly like some of the tests she would have written anyway for acceptance testing after the fact. Cindy realized that putting in the support code to get FIT (Framework for Integrated Tests) was not trivial—maybe even constituted too much work. She had to reluctantly admit that part of the difficulty in writing the support code is that she had to Refactor some business code that had made its way into the UI. Caleb, because he has been around this block before, is content—the work put in to get the FIT tests running improved the architecture of the system and paved the road for future changes as the system evolves.. The team recognized this problem on their own and had found a solution! The team was beginning to "grock" that Agile development is all about continuous improvement.

Context:

You are on a development project with a *Customer* who is willing and able to participate more fully as part of the development team. Your team is also willing to make difficult changes to any existing code. You are willing to pay the price of a high learning curve. Any of the following issues strengthens the fit of this pattern but are not necessary.

You are on a distributed development team with the requirements created at one location and the development done at another location.

You want to significantly reduce the bug count of your code.

You want to significantly reduce the time to market of your development team.

You want to build a system that solves the right problem and delivers more value to market (one of the business values in Part 1).

Forces:

The forces that are resolved by *Test-driven Requirements* are all of the forces that are resolved individually by the practices that make up this cluster. These forces are addressed more strongly by the cluster than the individual practices are:

- *Functional Tests* that are not part of a *Continuous Integration* build tend to fail silently. When they are discovered it is not obvious which check in (of the multiple builds that ran in the background via *Continuous Integration*) caused the problem. In this scenario *Functional Tests* may not all be passing because the feedback is not frequent enough. This reduces the quality improvement from *Functional Tests* and can lead to them becoming "second class" tests.

- *Customer Part of Team* without *Functional Tests* causes errors in translation between requirements and code. The *Customer* means one thing and the developer understands it as another.
- The previous point—errors in translation—is exacerbated with a distributed team where the *Customer* and the developer are not co-located. There are cultural differences that make this even worse.
- *Functional Tests* tend to fail silently and remain that way without *Continuous Integration*.

Therefore:

Have a *Customer Part of Team* that can work closely with developers to write *Functional Tests*. Have the *Customers* write their requirements as *Functional Tests* instead of your previous method. By doing this you will now have a concrete, unambiguous method of communication between *Customers* and developers even in distributed, multi-cultural teams. Also have *Continuous Integration* include not only *Automated Developer Tests* but all *Functional Tests* in each build. Use the tips in the *Functional Tests* pattern to run your tests fast enough for this to be feasible.

A developer's task is to build the part of the system that will satisfy the *Functional Tests* and build the needed scaffolding for the tests to execute correctly. Once the new *Functional Tests* are passing, the developer runs all of the *Automated Developer Tests* and all of the *Functional Tests* for the entire system locally and upon success checks in the new code into source control. Because *Functional Tests* are run by *Continuous Integration* then all of the requirements built so far by the entire team over all *Iterations* will be tested.

These practices, when used together as described, make up the *Test-driven Requirements* cluster. The requirements are written as tests and the same tight feedback loop found in *Test-driven Development* is expanded to include the entire team.

Adoption:

Adoption of course relies on the individual adoption of the practices. *Customer Part of Team* should be adopted before *Functional Tests*. *Continuous Integration* can be adopted at any time. *Test-driven Requirements* requires more than just the three practices to be adopted. You must actively work to thread them together:

1. For *Functional Tests* to really be used as requirements the *Customer* must learn to write the tests and this is usually a process that takes time. It also frequently requires help from a technical person, frequently testers from the QA team or developers can pair with the *Customer* for several *Iterations* until it becomes natural. (See the *Functional Tests* pattern for more details.)
2. The second part is that a "language" forms between the *Customer and the* developers via the tests. This is a step-wise process. Plan that this language will evolve as these practices are adopted together.
3. Do your best to make all *Functional Tests* run with every build in *Continuous Integration*. These tests are slower than *Automated Developer Tests* and will need more care to keep them running fast enough without causing *Continuous Integration* to break down.

But:

Like the other technical clusters, *Test-driven Requirements* depends on all of its practices to be executed well. If any of the three practices have problems this affects the cluster—therefore check the *But* section of *Functional Tests, Continuous Integration,* and *Customer Part of Team.*[12]

The most common problem is that of *Functional Tests* running slowly. This causes two problems:

*   Developers will not run all tests before checking in. Therefore *Continuous Integration* is more likely to break on check-in.

---

[12] Customer Part of Team is not documented in this book, so unfortunately you will have to go elsewhere for problems with this practice.

- The *Continuous Integration* build will be slow and test will fail without a clear indication of who should fix the broken tests.

In order to get *Functional Tests* into the *Continuous Integration*, the tests must be made fast enough. First, the team must make a commitment to functional testing as a primary development practice instead of a secondary one. When it is not an option to drop the tests, then teams find creative solutions. The main thing is to speed up the running of the *functional tests* so they can be run effectively by developers on their local machines before checking in. Here are some effective strategies to help you speed up your tests:

- *Functional Tests on Separate Machines:* By grouping tests into related suites, each suite can easily be run on its own machine. This effectively parallelizes the test suite and can give a speed increase proportional to the number of machines used.
- *Functional Tests Rollback Database Transaction:* This is a very simple but effective idea: don't commit your database transactions if you are testing end-to-end. We have seen this practice emerge independently on different projects and this usually gives about an order of magnitude increase in speed.
- *Functional Tests Refactored to Thinner Slices:* By testing a small scenario within each test instead of several scenarios (or even all scenarios) for a use case we get a finer granularity for splitting up tests. We have also found that larger tests tend to have more redundancy—breaking them up allows for faster individual tests.
- *Functional Tests Grouped By Business Area:* Grouping *functional tests* by business area allows a developer to test the subset of relevant tests on their machine without running the full suite. This allows for a faster red-green-red test loop and will keep a test suite from slowing the pace of development.

Note that having independent database sandboxes for each functional test run is a prerequisite for the above advice. If two *functional tests* run against the same database, one may report an incorrect "failure" because of interactions with the data inserted by the other test.

Variations:

Test-driven Requirements using xUnit Tests when the *Customer* is technical. With a technical *Customer* tests as code may be more appropriate and natural than a spreadsheet-like solution with FIT and FITNesse. This technique can be seen as a smell instead of a valid variation if the *Customer* doesn't write these tests but 'tells' the developer what to do.

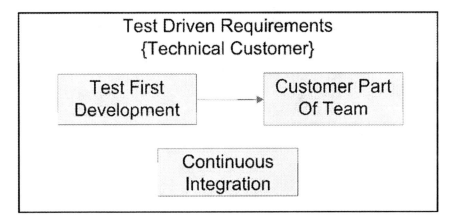

References:

Ron Jeffries uses "Running Tested Features" as an important metric for tracking project progress. These are the *Functional Tests* used with *Continuous Integration.*

Jeffries, Ron. "Running Tested Features."
   http://www.xprogramming.com/xpmag/jatRtsMetric.htm.

Joshua Kerievsky describes a practice almost identical to *Test-Driven* Requirements which he has named *Story-Driven Development.*

Kerievsky, Joshua. "Don't Just Break Software, Make Software."
   http://www.industriallogic.com/papers/storytest.pdf .

Conclusion

You made it to the end of the book—congratulations to both of us!

My hope is that you have created an initial Agile practice adoption strategy tailored to your development team, environment, and organization. Remember to adopt incrementally and make sure that the practices you are adopting to increase business value or alleviate a smell are having their intended effect. You are well on your way to building better software.

If you have not created an adoption strategy then I hope you have found the patterns and clusters useful to your current efforts to use Agile practices. You can find more advice on using the patterns in stand-alone format in the appendices Getting the Most from Agile Practice Patterns and Reading a Pattern Effectively.

I realize that there are many more Agile practices that have not been discussed. The appendix Patterns of Agile Practices Referenced but Not Defined contains short descriptions of other practices. There are also more practices and clusters that are in the works. Look for a follow-up to this book later in 2007 to elaborate and expand upon the set of patterns and clusters here.

Remember to treat these patterns with a modicum of disrespect. The pattern format is an excellent format to help you tailor your own solution. Every one of these patterns is based on multiple projects using the practices. They are proven in the field several times over. Nevertheless, there is no silver bullet. These patterns will be wrong in some instances. Use these patterns as guidance, but when reality contradicts theory—choose reality.

Finally, if you would like incremental information about the work being done with patterns of Agile practice adoption, the latest information will always be available at http://www.elssamadisy.com.

Appendices

17

Pattern to Business Value Mappings

The clusters and practices in each cell are ordered according to their effectiveness with respect to the given business value. Therefore, if you were to address "reduce time to market" you would consider adopting Simple Design before you considered Functional Tests.

Practices and Clusters that Improve Business Value

Business Value	Clusters of Agile Practices	Agile Practice Patterns
Reduce time to market	Test-driven Development, Evolutionary Design, Test-driven Requirements	Simple Design, Refactoring, Test-First Development, Test-Last Development, Continuous Integration, Functional Tests
Increase value to market	Test-driven Requirements	Functional Tests
Increase quality to market	Test-driven Development, Test-driven Requirements, Evolutionary Design	Test-First Development, Test-Last Development, Refactoring, Simple Design, Continuous Integration

157

Increase flexibility	Evolutionary Design, Test-driven Development, Test-driven Requirements	Automated Developer Tests, Refactoring, Collective Code Ownership, Functional Tests
Increase visibility	Test-driven Requirements	Functional Tests, Continuous Integration
Reduce cost	Evolutionary Design, Test-driven Development, Test-driven Requirements.	Simple Design, Refactoring, Collective Code Ownership, Test-First Development, Test Last Development, Functional Tests
Increase product lifetime	Test-driven Development, Evolutionary Design, Test-driven Requirements	Refactoring, Automated Developer Tests, Functional Tests, Simple Design

18

Pattern to Smell Mappings

The clusters and practices in each cell are ordered according to their effectiveness with respect to the given smell. Therefore, if you were to address "Quality delivered to customer is unacceptable" you would consider adopting Test-First Development before Continuous Integration.

Practices and Clusters that Alleviate Smells

Smell	Clusters of Agile Practices	Agile Practice Patterns
Quality delivered to customer is unacceptable	Test-driven Development, Test-driven Requirements, Evolutionary Design	Test-First Development, Test-Last Development, Refactoring, Simple Design, Continuous Integration
Delivering new functions to customer takes too long	Test-driven Development, Evolutionary Design, Test-driven Development	Simple Design, Refactoring, Test-First Development, Test-Last Development, Continuous Integration, Functional Tests

Features are not used by customer	Test-driven Requirements	Functional Tests
Software is not useful to customer	Test-driven Requirements	Functional Tests
Software is too expensive to build	Evolutionary Design, Test-driven Development, Test-driven Requirements.	Simple Design, Refactoring, Collective Code Ownership, Test-First Development, Test Last Development, Functional Tests
Us vs. Them	Test-driven Requirements	Functional Tests
Customer asks for everything including the kitchen sink	Test-driven Requirements	Functional Tests
Customer? What customer?!	Test-driven Requirements	none
Management is surprised	Test-driven Requirements	Functional Tests
Bottlenecked resources		Collective Code Ownership

Churning projects	Test-driven Development, Test-driven Requirements	Automated Developer Tests, Functional Tests, Continuous Integration
Hundreds of bugs in bug-tracker	Test-driven Development, Test-driven Requirements	Automated Developer Tests, Functional Tests, Continuous Integration
Hardening phase needed		Continuous Integration
Integration is infrequent		Continuous Integration

19

Adoption Strategy Case Study[13]

Introduction

It's all too easy to get caught up in the energy of trying out new Agile practices like pair programming, iterative development, and test-driven requirements, and lose sight of the original motivating factors behind instituting those practices in the first place. There may be this vague notion that "anything new has got to be better than what we have always (often painfully) done around here," and therefore the mere fact that you are trying something new is often good enough to justify the investment in time and effort of adopting a new practice. Yet at the same time, there are now so many practices which fall under the Agile umbrella that you may find yourself trying to figure out how you can possibly adopt everything at once, because maybe that one practice you ignore could be the one that makes the biggest difference. One popular way of dealing with this madness is by picking one particular methodology or set of practices and internalizing them (or at least promoting them) to the point that your software development organization becomes an "XP shop" or a "Scrum shop" or a "UP shop." For every team member plus half the marketing team and a few of the more enlightened senior managers, purchase a copy of your Agile Methodology Adoption book of choice, agree on a few minor details such as the time and place for your new daily standups and which *Continuous Integration* tool to use, and you are well on your way to becoming a full-blown Agile Development Shop.

---

[13] This article has been reprinted here with the approval of InfoQ and the authors.

While this is a common and useful approach, it's unfocused and tends to result in behavioral change simply for the sake of change. There is, however, a more targeted approach to Agile practice adoption that does not promote one particular named methodology over another but rather helps you pick and choose those practices that will best help you achieve your organizational goals. The following three points summarize this approach:

- It is all too easy to forget who the real customers are.
- Change for the sake of change tends to dilute the results of becoming Agile.
- You don't need to adopt every popular Agile practice to see a positive change, but rather a focused, diagnostic approach will help get you where you want to go faster and easier.

For this article we will consider the ongoing work of the BC 2.0 team. This is a development team that is working to rewrite a successful website that has millions of hits per day. We will share how we went about identifying which Agile practices would be most beneficial to adopt. The approach we took was to start by prioritizing a comprehensive list of possible business values to highlight those specific business values that the team felt most accurately represented what they were trying to accomplish with the BC 2.0 development effort. We then talked about which Agile practices are most closely aligned to each of their top three desired business values and found that a few key practices either influenced or provided the basis on which many others depend. Finally we discussed which of those Agile practices the team was currently utilizing and, based on that, crafted a plan for adopting the remaining high-impact practices.

Crafting an Agile Practice Adoption Strategy

Determine Business Value

The first step, regardless of where the team is today, is to focus on the business values that they are trying to bring to their customers. This actually required a slight step back to first identify who the customers were for, as with so many public websites whose revenue is based on advertising sales, the end user of the site is rarely the actual source of income for the company. With this understanding, we went through an exercise where we prioritized business values as understood by the development team. This question must again be asked of the customers of BC 2.0 which will include members of advertising, publishing, and management. At this point here is a first cut of the business values in prioritized order:

1. Value to Market/ Product Utility
2. Quality to Market
3. Visibility (to Customer)

There are possibly other business values that are important to the company such as:

4. Reduce Cost
5. Flexibility (turn on a dime)
6. Time to Market
7. Product Lifetime

Of the three business values deemed important, by and large *Product Utility* is the most important to this group, meaning that their emphasis should be on delivering a useful website as determined by the end users. Delivering a high quality website and keeping their customers informed of ongoing changes were also high on their list of important business values. What's even more telling about this particular organization is the list of business values that were considered lower priority. At many companies, reducing cost, delivering quickly, and building a long-life product are key goals, which understandably should influence the practices that they adopt. However their focus on building a high-quality, useful site means that they will want to emphasize different aspects of their development effort, specifically those that deal with customer involvement and feedback.

Focus Activities and Technologies toward Business Values

This next recommendation seems obvious, but in truth is something we, the software development community, have never done well:

drive the use of process and technology by business value. This means, if a practice or technology cannot be related to business values as prioritized by the customer or organization, it should not be used.

Here is a list of software development practices to consider (for all business values):
1. Test-First Development
2. Test-Last Development
3. Evolutionary Design (cluster)
4. Upfront Design
5. Upfront Architecture
6. Upfront Requirements
7. Refactoring
8. Continuous Integration
9. Simple Design
10. Collective Code Ownership
11. Test-driven Development (cluster)
12. Functional Tests
13. Test-driven Requirements(cluster)
14. *Iteration*
15. Stand Up Meeting
16. Retrospective
17. Pair Programming
18. Kick Off Meeting
19. User Story
20. Use Case
21. Information Radiator
22. Customer Part of Team
23. Evocative Document
24. Prioritized Backlog
25. Demo

Of the practices listed above, here are the ones currently practiced by the team:
1. Upfront Architecture
2. Upfront Requirements
3. Continuous Integration

4. Functional Testing (beginning stages)
5. *Iteration*
6. Retrospective
7. Kickoff
8. User Story
9. Collective Code Ownership

To help us determine which practices should be introduced or emphasized, we used the following Agile practice dependency maps for each of the three business values we are interested in. Each of these diagrams shows the practices that affect that business value and their interdependencies.

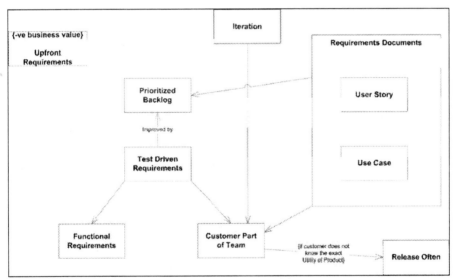

4 Product Utility Practices

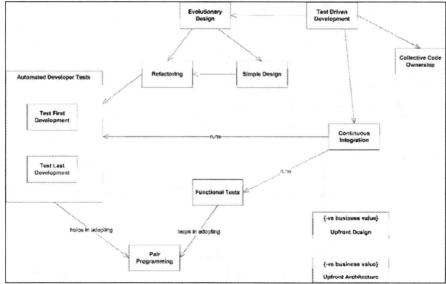

5 Product Quality Practices

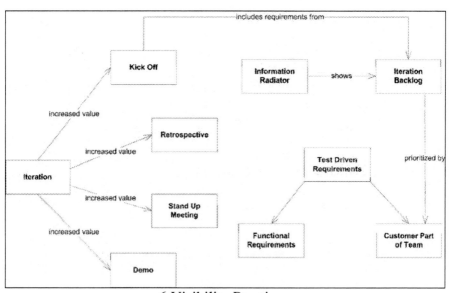

6 Visibility Practices

Based on the business value priorities, the practices in the above diagrams should be incrementally adopted, starting with any key practices that either influence many others or have a number of practices which depend on them.

All of the practices currently adopted (except *Upfront Architecture*) directly to address the high priority business values described above. Those practices should be kept and the Upfront Architecture and Upfront Requirements should be diminished because they cannot be realistically dropped. At this point we have a large list of practices we want to adopt and a couple that we would like to diminish. It is almost never a good idea to take a large number of practices at once; an incremental adoption strategy is better.

So which practices, of all the practices listed should be adopted? We started with the most important business value, *Product Utility*. Within the practices listed in *Product Utility*, we took the practices with the most incoming dependencies because they enable other practices. This leads us to:

- Customer Part of Team
- Release Often
- Automated Functional Tests

When we take a look at the next business value, *Product Quality,* we pull in Automated Developer Tests because many other practices depend on their presence and Pair Programming to support its adoption.

- Pair Programming
- Automated Developer Tests

From the third business value in our list we pulled a simple stand-alone practice to adopt:

- Information Radiators

When the team has successfully adopted these practices they will go back and pull in more practices to increase the business value they deliver. A practical adoption strategy includes an iterative approach to incorporating new practices, in other words: Adopt in small steps. The BC 2.0 group will begin with these practices and learn as they go. They need to experience the practices for themselves and build up their own body of experience. After an adoption cycle or two, they should revisit their list of business values to see if any have changed or been noticeably addressed. In addition to their end-of-*Iteration Retrospectives,* they should also periodically review the progress and feedback from their adoption efforts, and use that as a steering influence for continued improvement.

Conclusions

The software development organization was more heavily focused on delivering usability and quality, which is a bit unusual in this age of almost relentless cost cutting and emphasis on time to market. Yet the development team was a fairly typical case from the standpoint of practice adoption, taking a hybrid approach of formally adopting Scrum while also incorporating individual Extreme Programming practices such as Continuous Integration and User Stories, in a piecemeal fashion as opposed to taking on the entire suite of XP practices. While there is certainly nothing wrong with this configuration, we want to promote the idea that certain practice groupings can result in specific business value improvements, and therefore teams looking for the most "bang for their buck" should pick those practices that align well with the driving forces behind their software development efforts.

Further Reading

This is a practical example of creating an adoption strategy tailored to a specific development team and project. The mini-book, *Patterns of Agile Practice Adoption: The Technical Practices*, take a much more involved and detailed look at creating an adoption strategy and incrementally adopting many of these Agile development practices.

Amr Elssamadisy and John Mufarrige   January 14, 2007
amr.elssamadisy@valtech.com and john.mufarrige@valtech.com

20

Patterns of Agile Practices Referenced But Not Defined

To keep the book short and to release it early only a small subset of the Agile practices were fully defined. There are many more Agile practices and useful clusters to be documented in pattern format—look for more of them later in 2007. With that said, here is a list of practices that have been referenced throughout the book but have not yet been documented as full patterns. If you would like incremental information about the work being done with patterns of Agile practice adoption, the latest information will always be available at http://www.elssamadisy.com .

Pattern	Description
Customer Part of Team	The customer (or a proxy such as a business analyst) is part of the development team. A customer interacts with the developers and testers to meet the goals of the project. Ideally, the customer is collocated with the developers.
Information Radiator	A document, poster, web page, or device that is placed in a location where members of the team will see the information constantly. They are used to convey important information to help team members make the good decisions. They are used to create an Agile work environment.
Iteration	A set time period where the team commits to a set goal and works without interruption to meet that goal. The goal should always be a

	demonstrable working subset of the system.
Pair Programming	Two people working together to develop software at the same machine. This typically results in higher quality code and more discipline in practices and information transfer and knowledge.
Retrospective	A meeting at the end of every cycle (*Iteration, Release, etc.*) where the team reflects on what went well and what did not. The resulting feedback from a retrospective should lead to modification of the software development process and practices to deliver more business value in the future.
Standup Meeting	The development team meets daily for 10–15 minutes to review the prior day's progress and bring up roadblocks for resolution.

21

Getting the Most From Agile Practice Patterns

Part 1 of this book addresses how to go about setting your goals and choosing the appropriate practices to achieve them. Once you have them, the following questions should be answered explicitly. If they are not answered explicitly the team will find itself answering them implicitly as it stumbles along. For the set of questions below assume that the team will adopt Practice A:

1. Where does Practice A fit within an adoption strategy? Does it come first? Do we introduce it a few months after getting warmed-up with other practices?
2. Which development practices are related to *Practice A*? Are there any prerequisite practices for *Practice A* to be effective? Is *Practice A* a prerequisite to other practices? Is *Practice A* a part of a cluster of related development practices that have a value as a whole much greater than the sum of its parts?
3. Should *Practice A* be adopted in stages or in one step? Are there any special mechanics to help adopt *Practice A?*
4. Are there any pitfalls to be wary of when adopting *Practice A*? Can something go wrong? What does it look like? What does it *smell* like? What are the symptoms when *Practice A* goes wrong?
5. Are there circumstances where *Practice A* should not be adopted?
6. Can *Practice A* be adapted to other forms without changing its substance? What *is* its substance anyway?

7. Are there any assumptions about values shared by the team that are necessary for *Practice A* to be effective?
8. Finally, consistent with the spirit of Agility, what *business value* does *Practice A* bring to a development team?

All of the above questions matter. All of the above questions should be asked when a team decides to adopt a development practice. Some of the answers to these questions are far from obvious. However, most of these questions can be succinctly answered using this book.

22

Reading a Pattern Effectively

The patterns I've written here have a natural level of overlap. This is not by accident. Removing the overlap would affect the readability of these patterns individually.

There is also a natural redundancy within each pattern. The *Forces* section lists the problems that are resolved by the pattern. The *Therefore* section resolves those problems and refers to those forces in doing so. Frequently, the *But* section discusses breakdowns in the practice that lead back to the original forces. Finally, the *Adoption* section overlaps with the *Therefore* section because they describe different aspects of the same practice.

There are different ways to use the patterns in this book and many of them involve skipping around within a pattern itself. The redundancy supports this skipping around mode of reading. I hope you will agree with me that the redundancy, although sometimes annoying, is better than the alternative of having to flip pages to tie different parts together.

There are several ways to read a pattern. Here are some ways that the patterns can be used depending on the situation:

- I am already practicing the pattern. There are no problems. I just want to see how others have used the same pattern.
  - Look up the pattern by name.
  - Read the context to see if you are using the pattern in the same environment as others have done.

175

- o Read the *Therefore* and *Variation* sections to match to the way you are using the practice.
- I am practicing a pattern but it doesn't seem to be very useful. Am I incorrectly using the pattern? Or is the pattern just not useful in my environment?
  - o Look up the pattern by name.
  - o Read the *Context* section If your environment doesn't match the context then maybe you should consider modifying the practice or dropping it all together.
  - o Read the *Forces* section. Are you trying to solve the same type of problems? If not then consider that the practice might be working but that you need another practice to solve the problems you have in mind.
  - o Check out the *But* section. You will find how others have gone wrong and get some advice on correcting the problems to get the full benefits from the practice.
- I have problems on my team that I want to solve by adopting Agile practices.
  - o Go back to the chapter on smells and try to match your problems to smells.
  - o Read the practice(s) that address that smell.
  - o For each practice
    - ▪ Read the context and make sure it applies to your environment.
    - ▪ Read the rest of the pattern.
    - ▪ If you decide to adopt the practice then follow the advice in the Adoption section.
    - ▪ Periodically check for any of the smells documented in the *But* section.
- I couldn't find the problems I want to solve in the Smells chapter. Does that mean that none of the practices can help?
  - o No. Read the forces of the individual patterns and see if you can find similar problems to the ones you want to address. You will probably find a match.
- We are adopting a particular practice. Are we there yet? Have we successfully used the pattern to its fullest?
  - o Find the practice pattern by name.

o Check the *Forces* section. Are any of the problems in the forces still problems on your team?

o Check the *But* section. Are any of the smells in that section present? If so address them.

o If none of the problems occur then you have gone beyond what is documented in this book. You probably have enough experience and intuition to tailor the patterns on your own. Congratulations!

Bibliography

Astels, David. *Test-Driven Development: A Practical Guide.* Upper Saddle River, NJ: Prentice Hall, 2003.

Beck, Kent. *Extreme Programming Explained: Embrace Change.* Addison-Wesley Professional, 1999.

Beck, Kent and Cynthia Andres. *Extreme Programming Explained: Embrace Change. Vol.2.* Addison-Wesley Professional, 2004.

Beck, Kent. *Test-Driven Development By Example.* Boston, MA: Pearson Education , 2003.

Feathers, Michael. *Working Effectively with Legacy Code,* Upper Saddle River, NJ: Prentice Hall, 2005.

Fowler, Martin. *Refactoring: Improving the Design of Existing Code.* Addison-Wesley Professional, 1999.

Fowler, Martin. *Continuous Integration.* http://www.martinfowler.com/articles/continuousIntegration.html .

Gandhi, P., N. Haugen, M. Hill, and R. Watt. "Creating a Living Specification Document with FIT." http://www.Agile2005.org/XR22.pdf.

Jeffries, Ron. *Extreme Programming Adventures in C#.* Redmond, WA: Microsoft Press, 2004.

Jeffries, Ron. Running Tested Features. *http://www.xprogramming.com/xpmag/jatRtsMetric.htm* .

Kerievsky, Joshua. *Refactoring to Patterns.* Addison-Wesley Professional, 2004.

Kerievsky, Joshua. Don't Just Break Software, Make Software. http://www.industriallogic.com/papers/storytest.pdf .

Marick, Brian. "Bypassing the GUI." *Software Testing and Quality Engineering* (September / October 2002): 41–47.

179

Martin, Robert, C. *Agile Software Development: Principles, Patterns, and Practices*. Upper Saddle River, NJ: Pearson Education, 2003.

Massol, Vincent. *JUnit in Action*. Greenwich, CT: Manning Publications, 2004.

Mugridge, R., and W. Cunningham. *FIT for Developing Software: Framework for Integrated Tests*. Upper Saddle River, NJ: Pearson Education, 2005.

Rainsberger, J.B. *JUnit Recipes: Practical Methods for Programmer Testing*. Greenwich, CT. Manning Publications, 2004.

Shore ,Jim. "A Vision For Fit." http://www.jamesshore.com/Blog/A-Vision-For-Fit.html.

About the Author

Amr Elssamadisy is a software practitioner—meaning he serves multiple roles on different teams including coach, instructor, developer, architect, tech-lead, Scrum master, project manager, etc. He is extremely passionate about building great software. It is creative, challenging, frustrating, and ultimately very rewarding. That is why he is so gung-ho about Agile development practices—because when applied correctly, they do marvels for development teams' results.

Ever since being introduced to eXtreme Programming in late 1999 at ThoughtWorks he has been sold (and as a consultant has been selling it to clients). As of the publication date of this book, Amr has completed seven full years of working exclusively with Agile practices, helping teams adopt and adapt practices to suit their environments and build better software.

Amr currently serves Valtech as a Principal Consultant where he helps Valtech's clients build better software using the latest technologies, and of course, adopting and adapting Agile practices.

On a more personal note, Amr enjoys the simple pleasures of life: family, food, music, and video games. He can be reached at http://www.elssamadisy.com

Printed in the United States
116719LV00004B/56/A